M000202286

The California Wildlife Habitat Garden

The California Wildlife Habitat Garden

HOW to ATTRACT BEES,
BUTTERFLIES, BIRDS, and
OTHER ANIMALS

by NANCY BAUER

A PHYLLIS M. FABER BOOK

UNIVERSITY OF CALIFORNIA PRESS

Berkeley   Los Angeles   London

University of California Press, one of the most distinguished university presses in the United States, enriches lives around the world by advancing scholarship in the humanities, social sciences, and natural sciences. Its activities are supported by the UC Press Foundation and by philanthropic contributions from individuals and institutions. For more information, visit www.ucpress.edu.

University of California Press
Berkeley and Los Angeles, California

University of California Press, Ltd.
London, England

Produced by Phyllis M. Faber Books
Mill Valley, California

© 2012 by The Regents of the University of California

ISBN: 978-052-026781-7
Library of Congress Control Number: 2011936604

Book design and typesetting by Beth Hansen-Winter
Text: Cochin and Futura
Display: Skylark ITC
Printing and binding: Global Interprint, Inc., Santa Rosa, CA
Manufactured in China

21   20   19   18   17   16   15   14   13   12
10   9   8   7   6   5   4   3   2   1

The paper used in this publication meets the minimum requirements of ANSI/NISO z 39.48-1992 (R 2002) (*Permanence of Paper*).

Photographer Pat Hunt can be contacted at pat@pathunt.net.

p. i: Birds use grasses and other plant material for building nests. Pictured here is a California Towhee. PHOTOGRAPH BY ROBERT WATKINS.

p ii: There are many quiet places to watch birds and other wildlife in the Adler garden (see Garden Profile, p. 18). PHOTOGRAPH BY MARYBETH KAMPMAN.

p. iv-v: Purple coneflowers (*Echinacea purpurea*) provide both nectar and landing platforms for butterflies. Mustard greens, gone to seed, provide food for birds. PHOTOGRAPH BY CINDY LAMAR.

p. vi: Stream sedge (*Carex nudata*) offers cover and foraging sites for birds and other wildlife near the pond in the Adler garden (see Garden Profile, p. 18). PHOTOGRAPH BY MARYBETH KAMPMAN.

Contents

Acknowledgments

I am fortunate that Charlotte Torgovitsky, friend and fellow traveler on the habitat gardening journey, generously shared her knowledge and experience as a wildlife gardener and educator. Her invaluable support, contributions, and research enriched this book in countless ways. I am extremely grateful that her friends Mieko and Bob Watkins, whose superb photographic skills contributed so immensely to this book, jumped in from the beginning and stayed the course. I am equally grateful to Bob Stewart, who generously shared his amazing collection of butterfly and insect photos and from whom I've learned so much over many years. I'm indebted to Kathy Biggs who not only shared her pond, photos, and expertise as a dragonfly expert, but also offered technical support whenever I needed it. My heartfelt thanks to the wildlife habitat gardeners who offered their gardens or stories or plant lists and photos: Judy Adler, Ken and Rhonda Gilliland, Susan Gottlieb, Charlotte Torgovitsky, Barbara Schlumberger, Donna Grubisic, Kathy and Dave

Biggs, Cynthia LaMar, Paul and Harmina Mansur, Stephanie Pacheco (and Nancy Heuler for her photos), Mike and Jolee Steinberg, Gloria Conley, Judy Brinkerhoff and Steve Harper, Lori Reeser, Jay Shields, Wendy Wittl and Greg Mohr, Marcia Basalla, Celia Kutcher, Larry Volpe, Wynne Wilson, Ken and Micky Shaw, Peter LaTourette, Ruth Troetschler, Louise Robinson, and David Long. Thanks to landscape designers Alrie Middlebrook and Kate Frey for sharing photos of their gardens and to photographers Pat Hunt, Mary Beth Kampman, Michael Creedman, and James Ho for their contributions and generous support. Carol Bornstein, Arvind Kumar, Melissa Pitkin, and Maile Arnold supplied contacts, and Jeff Caldwell, Donna Eagles, Susan Swartz, Frederique Lavopierre, Janice Alexander, and Wade Belew read chapters or offered information, insights, and comments. Special thanks to my daughter, Maya Creedman, whose sharp eye kept me honest and whose encouraging words kept me going. Finally, I wish to thank Phyllis Faber and book designer Beth Hansen-Winter, and the editors and staff of UC Press, for their skills and support in spreading the word.

The nest box in this wildlife garden provides a home for Barn Owls. PHOTOGRAPH BY MIEKO WATKINS.

Why Garden for Wildlife?

As a child I was lucky to have Nature as a friend. The long, smooth branch of an old sycamore that grew at the edge of our neighborhood creek was a favorite childhood place to mull things over. Milkweed grew in nearby fields and undeveloped lots, their fascinating seedpods leaking silky threads of dark seeds in the fall that floated off with the wind. Fat toads, butterflies, and fireflies were plentiful, though they were much harder to find when I returned with my daughters many years later. My love for Nature, for plants and wild animals, began in that midwestern town at a time when vacant lots, woods, and uncultivated fields were abundant and children had the freedom and time to explore.

Those memories resurfaced in the spring of 1994, long after I had moved to the San Francisco Bay Area, at a presentation on wildlife habitat gardening at the first Master Gardener conference held at the UC-Davis campus. Two of the presenters were Dr. Don Mahoney, horticulturist at the San Francisco Botanical Garden, and Barbara Deutsch, a well-known San Francisco butterfly habitat gardener.

Their compelling stories and images of vibrant gardens alive with birds and butterflies were all the inspiration I needed to jumpstart my own journey. It was Don who started me out with checkerbloom (*Sidalcea malviflora*), my first butterfly host plant, and Barbara, too, shared her wild and wonderful butterfly garden and years of experience. Within several weeks of planting the checkerbloom, tiny caterpillars of the West Coast Lady butterfly appeared. It was a thrilling moment, followed by two quick lessons in butterfly gardening: (1) if the host plant is small, you need more than one, and (2) butterfly caterpillars

Checkerbloom (*Sidalcea malviflora*) is a caterpillar food plant for the West Coast Lady butterfly.
PHOTOGRAPH BY MIEKO WATKINS.

OPPOSITE: A pedestal birdbath in the author's garden is a favorite watering hole for birds that forage in a hedgerow of *Rosa rugosa*, *Buddleia salvifolia*, and spice bush (*Calycanthus occidentalis*). PHOTOGRAPH BY NANCY BAUER.

have many enemies. I managed to hunt down additional plants, and (with a little additional help) several caterpillars pupated and successfully emerged. It was my first attempt at butterfly habitat gardening and I was completely and unequivocally hooked.

As it turns out there are other reasons to grow wildlife gardens other than for the joy of it. Though the West Coast Lady butterfly can

West Coast Lady butterfly.
PHOTOGRAPH BY
ROBERT WATKINS.

still be found in Bay Area gardens, it is not faring well elsewhere in northern California. "Populations of the once-abundant West Coast Lady," says Arthur Shapiro, University of California-Davis butterfly expert, "are down to about 10 percent of what they were 20 years ago in the southern Sacramento Valley," and the "once common Anise Swallowtail is teetering on the brink of regional extinction." Butterflies that were once routinely showing up in gardens—Acmon Blues, Tailed Blues, Purplish Coppers, and, even, Mourning Cloaks, says Shapiro, have disappeared not only from urban and suburban neighborhoods, but wild lands, too.

Even the Monarch, our most widely recognized butterfly, has been experiencing severe population declines. The World Wildlife Fund added the Monarch butterfly to its list of "10 to Watch in 2010," along with tigers, polar bears, rhinos, and other threatened species. It's not just butterfly species that are in trouble. Toads, frogs, bees, and some songbird species are disappearing, too, at alarming rates. While experts rarely agree on any one explanation for the decline of wildlife species, the rapid loss and degradation of habitat in California, and throughout the country, is a chief concern. Protected wilderness, which is a very small percentage of our total available land, provides only fragmented and isolated islands of habitat. Unprotected wildlife habitat continues to shrink due to roads, development, agriculture, and urban sprawl. In his book *Bringing Nature Home*, entomologist Douglas Tallamy gives notice: "It has become increasingly clear that much of our wildlife will not be able to survive unless food, shelter, and nest sites can be found in suburban habitats." And which plants we choose to grow, Tallamy points out, determines the diversity and the numbers of wildlife that a particular garden can sustain.

So, now it's up to us. When we create habitat—places for birds, butterflies, bees, and other wild creatures to live, find food, and reproduce—we are helping to restore a small part of what has been lost. These creatures are an integral part of our lives and the health of the plants we grow. They clean up excess seeds and bugs, pollinate our fruits, vegetables, and flowers, prevent disease in the garden, and fascinate us with their relationships to each other and with the plants they depend on for survival.

Each wildlife garden has its own unique cast of characters, each habitat gardener his or her own unique experiences. What is common to us all, however, is the irresistible urge to spend as much time in the garden as we can, walking among the plants, observing what's showing up and enjoying the action. Into my twelfth year in a rural setting in west Sonoma County, the garden has settled and matured, yet constantly changes. I tend an average-sized lot, anchored by a huge black oak, at the western edge of a much larger and diversely planted property that has been stewarded by the owners in an exemplary fashion. Instead of the deer herd I gardened with at my first home in Marin County, a marauding band of gophers comes with this territory. Through many failed plantings I have learned which plants they are likely to avoid and which ones are delectable. I use more gopher wire, do grumble a bit, and then look at the upside: they aerate the soil. Years of gardening with wildlife and with plants I love have changed me into a more patient, less "energetic" gardener. I exert less control, I prune lightly, and try to keep "rearranging" at a minimum.

Though I grow non-native habitat plants, which include edibles (berry bushes, herbs, and a small food garden), the focus is natives. Their beauty, rich fragrances, and textures weave together each section of the garden, making the garden whole. Each year, as more native plants are added, the bird and insect life increases. Native bees and hummingbirds feed on whorls of blue, pink, and white lavender-tinged salvia flowers from early spring into summer. Drifts of these four native species (purple sage, Brandegee sage, black sage, and hummingbird sage) are my reliable, look-good-in-any-season, no-care treasures. Hard-working evening primrose often chooses where it wants to be and I almost always go along with the plan. Bumblebees coated with pollen stagger from the sunny flowers from late spring into fall; finches do acrobatics on its stalks, feeding on its abundant seed for months. Birds feast on the fruit of coffeeberry, elderberry, native currants, hawthorne, and crabapple. Behind the veggie garden grows a stand of cow parsnip that blooms in the spring. Their white, flat-topped umbels that are so appealing to the tiniest of pollinators remind me of my favorite trail at the Sonoma coast where they grow in profusion. Hedgerows of trees and shrubs, drifts of perennials, vines, grasses, and wildflowers provide berries, seeds, nectar, and pollen through the year without fertilizers or special care and with very little supplemental water.

For many of us, wildlife habitat gardening is not so much a gardening style as a passion that arises from a love of Nature and Her creatures, beauty, wisdom, and design. Certainly one of the main reasons to garden for wildlife is for the joy of it, for the rewards, for the unexpected pleasures. One of my mine is looking up from the computer to see who's in the large earth-cast birdbath in the back garden. One warm sunny day last November I counted seven species—White-crowned and Golden-crowned Sparrows, a Hermit Thrush, a Spotted Towhee, a California Towhee, Bushtits, and a Song Sparrow—all vying for positions! Whether it's the California Towhee enjoying a long, luxurious bath or the quick communal bathing of Bushtits or the occasion line-up for a spot in the water, birdbath action is one of the most delightful perks of a wildlife garden.

I urge you to spend time in your gardens not only to plant or trim or pull weeds, but also to see the season's changes on each plant, to watch a butterfly sipping nectar or discover its tiny pearl of an egg on the backside of a leaf, to hear the hummingbird and bee working the blossoms, and to consciously inhale the fragrance of a flower. In the chapters that follow, California wildlife habitat gardeners share their gardens, their insights, and their own special pleasures and rewards. There are as many ways to create wildlife gardens as there are gardeners to envision them. Who will come and what will happen is the mystery; only the rewards are guaranteed.

When California was wild, it was one sweet bee-garden throughout its entire length, north and south, and all the way across from the snowy Sierra to the ocean. . . . The Great Central Plain of California, during the months of March, April, and May, was one smooth, continuous bed of honey-bloom, so marvelously rich that, in walking from one end of it to the other, a distance of more than 400 miles, your foot would press about a hundred flowers at every step. Mints, gilias, nemophilas, castilleias, and innumerable compositae were so crowded together that, had ninety-nine per cent of them been taken away, the plain would still have seemed to any but Californians extravagantly flowery.

—John Muir, *The Mountains of California* (1894) (Excerpted from *The Bee-Pastures*, published by Partners for Sustainable Pollination, 2009)

CHAPTER 1

Growing a Wildlife Garden

Sometimes the gardener is the director, sometimes a mere player,
but for the most part a habitat gardener is a spectator
expectantly awaiting the next twist or turn in nature's plot.

—Judy Adler, wildlife habitat gardener

What is your personal vision of the perfect garden? Does it come from a childhood memory? A photo spread in a gardening magazine? A botanical garden you've visited? Though our visions may differ, for decades the American landscape of lawn, trimmed shrubs, and neat flowerbeds has been the standard for most homeowners throughout the country. There is a new twenty-first-century vision of gardening afoot, however, that is quietly and steadily gaining momentum. This new paradigm views the garden as a living ecosystem rather than merely as outdoor decoration. It recognizes the intricate relationships between plants and wildlife and our changing role as steward, rather than manipulator, of these relationships. This gardening philosophy, which values individual creativity over conventional design, is often described as "natural gardening." It encompasses a variety of concepts and gardening styles that include biological diversity, ecological design, and environmentally friendly gardening methods.

Wildlife habitat gardening embraces all aspects of natural garden-

A Dark-eyed Junco enjoys a bath.
PHOTOGRAPH BY ROBERT WATKINS.

OPPOSITE: California wild grape (*Vitis californica* 'Roger's Red') provides a lush summer screen in Judy Adler's garden (see Garden Profile, p.18). PHOTOGRAPH BY MARYBETH KAMPMAN.

1

Bushtits bathe communally in this shallow birdbath. PHOTOGRAPH BY CINDY LAMAR.

ing with an additional emphasis on providing food, cover, and water for wildlife. Backyard gardens have become increasingly important as wildlife sanctuaries as agricultural practices, human development, and invasive plants have led to the destruction and degradation of wildlife habitat. Protected wilderness, those scattered and isolated islands of habitat, no longer are sufficient for sustaining wildlife, and the corridors that are needed for wildlife to move from one area to another are missing. "Our gardens," says entomologist and author Douglas Tallamy, "are the last chance we have for sustaining plants and animals that were once common throughout the United States." Wildlife gardens can provide the necessary food and shelter—resources that in the past were more available on undeveloped lands—that enable various wildlife species to get through all seasons, dry summers or cold winters.

There are many compelling reasons to create a wildlife garden, but "wanting to do something positive for the planet" and "personal pleasure" are among the reasons I most often hear. "We have the power as individual habitat gardeners," says Judy Adler, whose garden is profiled in this chapter, "to play a part in reversing the practices that have caused the degradation of many of the Earth's natural resources. I can't think of a more meaningful gift to the world." For most wildlife habitat gardeners the focus is on attracting birds, butterflies, bees and other beneficial insects. Songbirds, toads and frogs, honeybees and various native bee and butterfly species are the canaries in the coalmine. They have been facing population declines for decades. They are the ones

Indian mallow and silver bush lupine provide nectar for pollinators and seeds for birds in this southern California wildlife garden. PHOTOGRAPH BY SUSAN GOTTLIEB.

most in need of backyard habitat in cities, suburbs, and rural areas too. While many wildlife gardeners choose to welcome all visiting wildlife, others draw the line at deer. Regardless of the wildlife focus, however, one thing quickly becomes clear: when you plant for one, you plant for all. A diversity of plants brings insects. The supply of insects

Many wildlife species find cover, food, and nesting sites in

feeds the birds, toads, frogs, lizards, and the predaceous and parasitic insects we call "beneficials." Nectar flowers bring in hummingbirds, bees, butterflies, and other pollinators. Other food plants feed the butterfly caterpillar or provide seeds, berries, nuts, or fruits for birds,

which may, in turn, eat some of the caterpillars—and other desirable insects.

Often, a bird-habitat gardener begins to notice butterflies in the garden and soon adds butterfly nectar and host plants; the butterfly

oak woodland communities. PHOTOGRAPH BY MIEKO WATKINS.

Pollinators feed on the nectar of California lilacs in spring; birds eat the seeds and insects they attract. Pictured here is *Ceanothus* 'Concha'.

PHOTOGRAPH BY MARYBETH KAMPMAN.

gardener finds more hummingbirds in the garden and starts looking for plants attractive to hummers. Inevitably, both become fascinated by all of the creatures that show up. Wildlife habitat gardening has a wonderful tendency to escalate! By supporting these relationships among plants and wildlife, the wildlife gardener, in turn, reaps a multitude of rewards.

Food and Shelter

How do we turn our backyards—and front yards—into wildlife habitat? It's really quite easy; no special training or skills are required and it doesn't involve starting over. Except for that all-too-common American landscape of lawn and clipped shrubs that offers very little to wildlife, many garden landscapes meet at least some of the needs of birds, insects, and other creatures. But there are many ways to enhance the wildlife value of *any* garden. All animals—birds, mammals, amphibians, reptiles, and insects—need shelter, foraging sites, and places to nest and breed. Overlapping, vertical layers of trees, shrubs and ground plants provide wildlife species with many different options for shelter, foraging, and nesting. Leaf litter, logs, and brush piles, even small ones, provide shelter for insects, lizards, and salamanders, and good foraging sites for birds. A dead tree, or snag, is home to cavity nesters such as woodpeckers, wrens, bluebirds, and tree swallows. Wildlife gardeners take their cues from Nature. Wilderness areas that contain the most diverse animal species also contain the most diverse plant species. *Diversity* is Nature's key concept.

Trees and shrubs that produce seeds, berries, fruit, or nuts feed birds; nectar flowers attract butterflies, bees, and other pollinators.

TOP: *Lavatera assurgentiflora,* a native mallow, is a butterfly nectar and host plant. PHOTOGRAPH BY MIEKO WATKINS. BOTTOM: In the fall, the California wild grape produces fruit for birds. PHOTOGRAPH BY JUDY ADLER.

Ideally, our "plant shelters" do double duty as nectar and food plants and, in some cases, do extra duty as host plants for butterfly caterpillars. Our native California lilac (*Ceanothus* spp.) is a good example of a multifunctional habitat plant. The clusters of early spring flowers provide nectar for pollinators, especially native bees that are just emerging; the seeds and insects this plant attracts feed many birds; and its foliage serves as a caterpillar host plant for the Spring Azure, California Tortoiseshell, and several other butterflies. Its many forms, from trees to mounding groundcover, offer shelter, nesting, and foraging sites for birds, insects, and other wildlife. Oaks are habitat heroes. They provide places to breed for owls and hawks and small cavity nesters, such as chickadees and nuthatches; their acorns feed woodpeckers, jays, and squirrels. According to the California Oak Foundation, over 300 species of wildlife (birds, mammals, amphibians, and reptiles) use oak woodlands for food, cover, and nesting. Over 5,000 species of insects, including seven butterfly species, are also part of this web of life. Even the mistletoe that hangs from oak

Oaks are multifunctional habitat plants. PHOTOGRAPH BY MIEKO WATKINS.

branches feeds the caterpillars of the Great Purple Hairstreak and provides fruit for birds.

While cover and plants that provide food, pollen, and nectar are essential for any wildlife habitat garden, it is the geographical region that signals which food and nectar plants gardeners should choose. California, in most areas, is blessed with a Mediterranean climate: warm, dry summers and cool, wet winters, though as many Californians are well aware, winters are not always wet. Our climate is similar to the Mediterranean Basin, where the name comes from, and other regions of the world that include the southern tip of South Africa, southern and western areas of Australia, and central Chile. Plants from these regions easily adapt to California's climate, especially the less foggy areas inland from the coast. The plants best adapted to our climate and soils are the ones that have always lived here—our native plants. These are the plants that have evolved with our native wildlife species; they meet all of their nutritional needs for pollen and nectar, fruit, seeds, and nuts. Native plants attract the highest number of insects (including beneficial insects) and, for some butterfly species, they are the only caterpillar host plants. Hundreds of non-native food and nectar plants, drawn mostly from other Mediterranean climate regions, supplement this large and diverse palette of native plants that are easy to grow, without the need for fertilizers, insecticides, or regular summer water.

A California Wildlife Garden

We Californians live in a magnificent land of evergreen forests, oak woodlands, chaparral studded hillsides, bluffs, and bays—one of the most floristically diverse regions in the world. Our California native plants give Californians our most essential expression of place. They are versatile and beautiful in their own right, and they have a long and enduring relationship with our wildlife. It is not a coincidence that many native trees and shrubs bloom when the nectar of their blossoms is most needed in early spring and produce fruit and nuts when birds are the hungriest. The life cycles of many of our native wildlife have evolved in

The manzanita hedge (*Arctostaphylos densiflora* 'Howard McMinn') in Judy Adler's garden provides nectar for hummingbirds in late winter/early spring. PHOTOGRAPH BY MARYBETH KAMPMAN.

relationship to the flowering and fruiting seasons of our native plants. Insects pollinate many of the plants and birds eat the fruit and spread the seed in this mutually beneficial relationship.

The delicate bell-shaped flowers of manzanitas blooming in late winter are a critical source of nectar for Anna's Hummingbird, our year-round resident that nests as early as December. It is a time when food sources are scarce. The nectar flowers of willow, blue elderberry, coffeeberry, and many other native trees and shrubs follow in spring with berries, nuts, or seeds for birds in the fall. Native sages and wildflowers bloom from February through May followed by summer-blooming perennials offering nectar, pollen, and seeds for birds. In the fall, when most plants are fading, goldenrod, California fuchsia, and coyote bush come into bloom. In December, the red berries of the beautiful toyon, also called Christmas berry, are a favorite winter food source of robins, mockingbirds, and thrushes.

There are more than 6,000 native plants in California, some of them found nowhere else in the world. Probably only half that many are suitable for gardens, and these are finding their way into the nursery trade in greater numbers each year. While many native plants from one region of the state can be grown in another, local native plant communities are the first place to look for inspiration and potential plant choices. California's large native plant communities include forest, woodland, grassland, chaparral, coastal scrub, desert scrub, and alpine communities. Knowing which plant communities are dominant (or were historically dominant) in your area is valuable information for understanding not only which plants might naturally grow well in your garden, but also what other native plants, with similar requirements, might be well suited

Summer-blooming matilija poppies bring in many native bees and other pollinators.
PHOTOGRAPH BY SUSAN GOTTLIEB.

for your site. Native plants, however, do not always follow our designated categories—plant communities often overlap and plants from one community can sometimes be found in another.

The key to success with natives is matching their natural growing conditions to your site. While many native plants are drought tolerant, plants that grow by streams in shady forests will have different needs from chaparral plants that grow in dry, sunny, exposed sites. Plants that grow in the summer fog zone of coastal areas need more moisture than those from areas farther inland. Plants with frost intolerances that do well in southern California or mild winter areas farther north are not good choices for California microclimates that experience hard freezes. Most native plants require good drainage and benefit when planted on mounds or in raised beds. All drought-tolerant plants need water to get established; some may need occasional deep watering the first or second year, or longer. The most advantageous times to plant natives are late fall and winter. Winter rains encourage the deep roots that natives need to weather the summer drought season. Native plants should *not* be fertilized and heavy mulching is not necessary. Allow leaf litter to accumulate under native trees and shrubs, just as it would in natural conditions.

Perhaps one of the hardest concepts for transplanted Californians to accept is that summer is the quiet season for many native plants. Unlike the lush landscapes of the eastern half of the country where summer rains are the norm, a California garden is resting in more muted tones of russets and golds. Yes, there are native perennials—from asters, mints, and mallows to the tall evening primrose, with its large sunny flowers, and the California fuchsia, with its flaming color—that brighten the garden in summer and fall. However, the glory season for California native plants is spring. That spring, though, starts in late winter, when the eastern half of the country may still be under snow—and it extends well into summer. Later, in the fall, those same trees and shrubs, no longer in bloom, are feeding birds and other creatures with nuts, berries, seeds, and fruit. Summer is not the time to water naturally dormant plants, though some do, but to accept the quiet beauty of their natural seasonal cycles.

Native coral bells attract hummers and work well under oaks. Pictured here is *Heuchera micrantha* 'Old La Rochette'.
PHOTOGRAPH BY MIEKO WATKINS.

Mixing Natives and Ornamentals

While an all-native garden may be the ideal, a wildlife habitat garden does not have to be 100 percent native. Typically, wildlife habitat gardens contain a mix of native and compatible non-native food and nectar plants (including fruit and nut trees, berry bushes, medicinal and culinary herbs, vegetables) that bloom and set fruit in different seasons. Non-native food and nectar plants, especially those with long bloom periods, can both supplement peak bloom times of native plants and prolong spring flower-

ing through the summer months, when bees, butterflies, and other pollinators and beneficial insects are foraging. Summer-blooming non-natives from the mint family (such as sages, lavender, calamint, catmint, lemon balm, thyme) and the sunflower family (asters, cosmos, zinnias, coreopsis, blanket flower, for example) are good sources of nectar and pollen for honeybees, other pollinators, and beneficial insects. Plants from these families (which also include many California

The flowers of the strawberry tree (*Arbutus unedo*) attract butterflies and other pollinators, and birds like the edible fruit.

PHOTOGRAPH BY CINDY LAMAR.

natives) bloom over a long period; seeds from the composites provide food in the fall for finches, juncos, and other seed-eating birds. Choose single-flowered, old-fashioned plant varieties, especially composites such as sunflowers, zinnias, blanket flower, coreopsis, and marigolds. They are almost always more nectar- and pollen-rich than the over-hybridized versions, many of which are selected for ornamental traits or for growing in pots. The flowers of many medicinal and culinary herbs—chaste tree, rosemary, oregano, dill, valerian—are excellent nectar sources for all types of pollinators. Butterflies and bees flock to the flowers of strawberry tree (*Arbutus unedo*) and the broad pinkish tops of *Sedum* 'Autumn Joy' and *S. spectabile* in late summer. Red hot poker plant, bottlebrush, flowering maple (*Abutilon* spp.), and fuchsias, for example, are valuable plants for the hummingbird garden.

Hundreds of non-native food and nectar plants are compatible with our climate and with California natives. Your choice depends on your site, personal preferences, and which wildlife species you are trying to attract. Grow a diversity of plants, with an emphasis on natives, that bloom at different times of the year. Massing nectar plants, especially perennials and annuals, in drifts of just one plant variety is more attractive to butterflies and bees than planting only one or two of many different species.

All Wildlife Need Water

Water, the most essential of the four basic needs, is fundamental to animals and humans alike. Bathing, too, is a delightful ritual that we share with many wildlife species and there are a myriad of drinking and bathing-station options for the wildlife gardener to consider. Birds are

Keeping Birdbaths Mosquito-Free

Keeping birdbaths, saucers, and other watering holes clean and filled with fresh water is essential to the health of the wildlife using them. When birdbaths are rinsed out and refilled daily, it also keeps mosquitoes from breeding in the birdbath. Because mosquitoes can breed in small amounts of standing water, it is wise to empty birdbaths when leaving for more than several days. (It takes a mosquito five to seven days to develop from egg to adult.) Scrub out birdbaths on a regular basis to remove algae and other debris. Please do not add chemicals to birdbath water; they are harmful to birds and other animals.

especially fun to watch. A birdbath is an easy way to provide a year-round source of water and is one of the great pleasures of a habitat garden. Even a saucer filled daily with fresh water will not go unnoticed. Placed on the ground, deck, or tree stump, it becomes available to birds and small mammals. With the addition of several large river stones, sand, or pebbles, a shallow saucer becomes a watering hole for butterflies and small insects, which need moisture more than water. Be cautious with the placement of birdbaths. Place them near enough to shrubs or trees to offer birds a quick escape but not close enough to provide a hiding place for cats. Domestic and feral cats are a bird's worst nightmare: annual U.S. estimates for birds killed by cats range from two to four million birds a day. A tall pedestal birdbath or a saucer held securely in a mesh harness and hung from a tree limb may be the best option if there are cats nearby.

Moving water is highly attractive to birds. A re-circulating fountain, a mister, a waterfall, or a bamboo spout will attract not only more birds, but a more diverse group as well. A wildlife pond or stream will not only bring in many local and migrating birds, but may also attract native tree frogs, dragonflies, deer, foxes, and other nocturnal animals.

OPPOSITE: Many different bird species enjoy the fountain in this habitat garden. PHOTOGRAPH BY SUSAN GOTTLIEB.

Garden Profile

The Adler Garden, Walnut Creek, Contra Costa County

Judy Adler's suburban garden in the San Francisco Bay Area was one of the first backyard wildlife habitats to be certified by the National Wildlife Federation. In 1978 this 1/2-acre site at the base of the Mt. Diablo foothills was completely devoid of vegetation. Landscape architect Ron Lutsko, Jr., designed various small-scale habitats—a small redwood grove, fruit trees, perennial and herb borders, a manzanita hedge, and pond—to offer wildlife shelter and nesting places, perches, foraging sites, food, and a source of water year-round. Inspired by the plant communities in nearby Mt. Diablo State Park, Judy emphasized California natives for their ability to attract local and migrating bird and butterfly species, their low-water needs, and the sense of history and beauty they bring to a landscape.

Since its inception over three decades ago, this wildlife garden has experienced many changes. Of the original plantings, some failed to prosper and new plants were regularly added as Judy honed her skills at finding the right plants for the right place. Some of the original plants adapted to changes in light and space as nearby plants matured. The California wild grape (*Vitis californica* 'Roger's Red') that was planted along a fence, for example, eventually wound its way to the top of a 30-year old redwood tree as it began to get shaded out by its neighbors. Though the redwoods no longer need watering, Judy admits that her reason for planting them—to replicate the serenity of their natural coastal setting—was not compatible with her hot inland microclimate. As she evolved as a gardener, lowering water consumption and gardening more sustainably became a high priority.

In recent years, as the garden focus shifted to edibles, the small backyard lawn was removed to make room for vegetable beds and

The pond and boardwalk are a gathering place for wildlife—and garden visitors.
PHOTOGRAPH BY MARYBETH KAMPMAN.

Garden Profile

additional fruit trees. Over 10 percent of the total plants in this garden (40 fruit trees, grape and kiwi vines, berry bushes, and vegetables) provide food for the owner (and the larger community) as well as the local wildlife that share in the bounty. The wildlife pond, a focal point of the garden since its beginnings, features a boardwalk that connects front and back gardens and serves as a viewing platform for observing aquatic life and other action on the pond. As a source of water for bathing and drinking, the pond is a magnet for birds, dragonflies, frogs, and small mammals that visit the garden. Boulders and rocks throughout the garden provide sunbathing sites for lizards and butterflies. Brush piles in corners, plant trimmings snuggled under shrubs, a few snags, and old logs provide shelter and additional places for birds to forage. As they decay, these organic materials enrich the microbial layers of the soil that are so important to plant health.

In the front garden the manzanita hedge (*Arctostaphylos* 'Howard McMinn'), which receives no summer water, doubles as a privacy screen and cover for quail. In the spring, its pink, bell-shaped nectar flowers bring in Anna's Hummingbirds and many species of native bees. Clusters of plant combinations rather than formal flowerbeds appear throughout the garden. A valley oak is underplanted with coffeeberry, pink-flowering currant and native coral bells—each plant layer offering cover, food, and nectar. The oak's acorns in the fall attract squirrels and woodpeckers, which, along with other bird species, feed on the insects the oak attracts. Coffeeberry offers tiny, nectar-rich flowers in the spring followed by green berries that turn black by fall, and it serves as a caterpillar host plant for the Gray Hairstreak and Pale Swallowtail butterflies. Hummingbirds and bees are attracted to the long pink pendants of the currant (*Ribes sanguineum*) and the delicate, pale-pink flowers of native coral bells (*Heuchera* spp.), an ideal choice for under oaks and other areas of dry shade.

OPPOSITE: Creambush (*Holodiscus discolor*) grows under a big-leaf maple in Judy Adler's front garden. BELOW: In late spring, cream-bush blooms with fragrant clusters of nectar flowers. PHOTOGRAPHS BY MARYBETH KAMPMAN.

Garden Profile

Behind the manzanita hedge, creambush (*Holodiscus discolor*) grows under a big-leaf maple where virgin's bower (*Clematis lingusticifolia*) winds its way through the branches, displaying creamy, star-like blooms in early summer. In late spring, pollinators flock to the fragrant flower clusters of creambush, which also serves as a butterfly host plant for the Lorquin's Admiral, Spring Azure, and Pale Swallowtail butterflies. Nearby, native blue elderberry blooms later in spring with fragrant showy nectar flowers followed by tasty edible berries for birds. In the back garden the winter-blooming silk tassel bush (*Garrya elliptica*) serves many functions. The shrub's dense foliage offers cover, its dramatic, long greenish catkins attract native bees and hummingbirds when little else is blooming, and birds love the fruit. (*Note*: only female plants produce fruit; most available varieties are male plants for the showier catkins.) In this garden fruit trees, such as pineapple guava and citrus, serve both as privacy screens and nectar sources for pollinators when their flowers appear in spring. A red-flowering *Abutilon*, an ornamental shrub that is highly attractive to hummingbirds, offers nectar over many seasons. Native and non-native perennials and grasses scattered throughout the garden tie the layers together at the ground level.

Gradually, Judy has incorporated more native grasses — California fescue, Idaho fescue, three-awn grass — into the plantings in both front and back areas. Birds forage for seeds and insects among the grasses and use them for nesting materials. With its diverse mix of food and nectar plants — trees, shrubs, vines, perennials, and grasses — and a source of fresh water year-round, this 30-year-old suburban wildlife garden encapsulates all of the essential requirements of habitat. The many varied vertical layers of trees and shrubs provide shelter and nesting places; a diversity of food and nectar plants bloom and set seed and fruit throughout the seasons.

Wildlife focus: In this garden all species of wildlife are welcome, including salamanders, lizards and the infrequent deer or fox. Beneficial Pacific Gopher snakes are occasionally spotted. Among the many bird species that frequent the garden are Mockingbirds, Western Bluebirds, California and Spotted Towhees, Black Phoebes, Bushtits, and Yellow-

rumped Warblers. Raptors, such as Red-tailed Hawks, favor the tops of the redwoods as perch points. The tiny native Pacific Chorus frogs that breed in the pond sing nightly when the males are looking for mates, and every so often Judy uncovers a wandering frog under a flower pot in the plant nursery. Monarch, Common Buckeye, Mourning Cloak, Western Tiger Swallowtail, and Fiery Skipper butterflies are seasonal visitors. Judy grows showy milkweed (*Asclepias speciosa*) and narrowleaf milkweed (*A. fascicularis*) as caterpillar host plants for the Monarch. Other butterfly host plants include false indigo (*Amorpha* spp.), wild lilacs (*Ceanothus* spp.), various oaks, coffeeberry, pink-flowering currant, and creambush.

The pond: The pond was constructed with felt and rubber liners,

Birds love to bathe near the waterfall in Judy Adler's pond. PHOTOGRAPH BY MARYBETH KAMPMAN.

Garden Profile

water, and gravel. A boardwalk divides the pond into two sections, which makes it easy to observe dragonflies and damselflies, water boatmen and water striders, beetles, and other insects. It also keeps foot traffic away from the native sedge (*Carex nudata*) and rushes that rim the edges of the pond. Mosquito fish, native frogs, and dragonflies control mosquito larvae, and birds, such as Black Phoebes, perform insect patrol duty. When the old pond liner was replaced in the fall of 2010 the owner added boulders and a waterfall. Almost immediately a flock of migrating Cedar Waxwings flew in to investigate!

New garden feature: Wildlife habitat gardening tends to foster sustainable thinking, and in Judy's case it led to installing a rain harvesting system (three 3,000-gallon tanks, two smaller tanks, and several rain barrels) to supplement the irrigation system and to replace pond water lost to evaporation during the hot summer months.

Plant installation: Judy's contractor handled the hardscaping and installation of the larger plant specimens, but Judy planted many of the perennials and small shrubs herself and she maintains the garden. Trees were purchased in 5- and 15-gallon sizes; shrubs in 2- and 5-gallon sizes; and perennials and vines in 4-inch or 1-gallon pots. Generally, the smallest and healthiest-looking plants were chosen and planted in the fall. Plants were bought at native plant nurseries, botanical gardens, native plant sales, and local nurseries. However, in the past ten years Judy has propagated many of the plants that have been added to the garden.

Garden practices: Judy's principle, "nothing toxic enters and nothing organic leaves the site," sums up her approach to gardening. She composts religiously. She makes heavy use of mulch, but leaves some bare ground to encourage soil-nesting native bees to make her garden their home. In addition to organic materials generated on site, she uses grounds from local coffee houses and large quantities of wood chips, delivered by tree service companies free of charge on a regular basis. "After 30 years of composting routinely," says Judy, "I really see the difference in the soil from the heavy clay I started with in the beginning." The overhead and drip irrigation systems were tailored to the needs of each plant community. Plants are watered only as needed.

Judy has observed that some native plants shed yellow leaves around July when it begins to get hot, which is part of their normal cycle and does not indicate that the plant is dying or needs water. Instead of meticulously cleaning up the garden in the fall, Judy leaves a share for the birds. Stems harbor over-wintering insects and the rotting leaves provide great cover for caterpillars, insect eggs, and nests, and foraging grounds for birds from fall through the winter months.

Favorite habitat plants: "Manzanitas and valley oaks have been the big winners," says Judy, "and I'm particularly fond of creambush for its modest size, form, and the cover and nectar it provides, and because birds use the spent flowers for nesting materials." She cites pink-flowering current, matilija poppies, and native coral bells for their beauty and attractiveness to native bees and other pollinators. She is also fond of the shade-loving spice bush (*Calycanthus occidentalis*) because of its aromatic leaves, pleasing form, and the unusual maroon flowers and fruit. She finds the long greenish catkins of the silk tassel bush, the first to bloom in late winter, equally appealing. Judy is convinced that having a large number of flowering native trees, shrubs, and perennials, which attract bees and other pollinating insects, promotes fruit production in her garden. Of the ornamentals she has planted, Judy especially enjoys the lilacs and buddleias for their fragrance, hardiness, and their appeal to butterflies.

Rewards: One of Judy's gardening rewards is passing forward her passion for garden ecology to schoolchildren by offering hands-on classes in her own garden and on adjoining school property. Children study plant parts and life cycles, plant/insect associations, composting, and propagation. Judy also leads watershed walks and directs community restoration projects for youth along public trails. As school kids participate in Nature and garden activities, they use all of their senses to experience plants, soil, and wildlife. Judy believes that the emotional, intellectual, and spiritual well-being of a child is derived from direct experiences with Nature, a belief thoroughly supported by author Richard Louv in his remarkable book, *Last Child in the Woods*. What better place to make the connection with Nature than in a wildlife habitat garden?

Seckel pear, Nubiana plum, and other fruit trees line the flagstone walkway in Judy Adler's backyard garden. Drifts of hellebores attract bees from late winter into spring. PHOTOGRAPH BY MARYBETH KAMPMAN.

The Adler Garden Partial Plant List
*Native plants

Trees and Large Shrubs

Arbutus 'Marina'. Nectar flowers and fruit in the fall, smooth reddish brown bark, easier to grow than the native madrone

*Big-leaf maple (*Acer macrophyllum*). Deciduous tree for cover, nesting/foraging sites, best for large gardens

Butterfly bush (*Buddleia davidii*). Summer nectar flowers for butterflies, hummingbirds, other pollinators

*California hazelnut (*Corylus cornuta* var. *californica*). Deciduous, fast growing, edible nuts

*Coffeeberry (*Rhamnus californica*). Drought-tolerant evergreen shrub, nectar-rich flowers in spring, ripe berries for birds in fall, attracts beneficial insects, butterfly host plant

*Creambush (*Holodiscus discolor*). Understory deciduous shrub, nectar flowers in spring, butterfly host plant

*False indigo (*Amorpha californica*). Butterfly host plant

Flowering maple (*Abutilon* hybrid). Long bloom period, hummingbird favorite

*Manzanita hedge (*Arctostaphylos densiflora* 'Howard McMinn'). Dense cover, nectar in early spring; this species tolerates heavy clay soil

*Silk tassel bush (*Garrya elliptica*). Evergreen, nectar for pollinators, seeds and fruit for birds; male plants have showier catkins in winter

*Toyon (*Heteromeles arbutifolia*). Nectar flowers, red berries for birds in winter

*Valley oak (*Quercus lobata*). Cover, foraging, and nesting sites; attracts many insects, acorns in fall, butterfly host plant

*Western spice bush (*Calycanthus occidentalis*). Unusual seedpods, spicy-scented maroon flowers, beetle pollinated

Smaller Shrubs

* Black sage (*Salvia mellifera*). Spring bloom, very attractive to native bees
* Oregon grape (*Berberis aquifolium*). Evergreen, hardy, drought tolerant, yellow nectar flowers in spring, fruit for birds
* Pink-flowering currant (*Ribes sanguineum* var. *glutinosum*). Nectar for hummers and other pollinators, fruit for birds, butterfly host plant
* Snowdrop bush (*Styrax officinalis*). Fragrant white nectar flowers in late spring; hummingbirds/other pollinators

Perennials, Vines, and Grasses

* California fuchsias (*Epilobium* spp.). Bright orange or red tubular flowers in fall, hummingbird favorite
* California wild grape (*Vitis californica* 'Roger's Red'). Deciduous vine with crimson leaves in fall, nectar flowers for bees, purple fruit for birds
* Coral bells/Island alumroot (*Heuchera maxima*). Airy stalks of tiny flowers, hummingbirds/other pollinators, good choice for under oaks

Coreopsis spp. Summer flowers, nectar and pollen for bees and beneficial insects, seeds for birds

Mexican sage (*Salvia leucantha*). Fall bloom, hummingbird favorite

* Narrowleaf milkweed (*Asclepias fascicularis*), showy milkweed (*A. speciosa*). Summer-

blooming nectar plants for butterflies and other pollinators; butterfly host plant

Penstemon spp. Spring through summer nectar flowers for hummers and other pollinators; may be used by the Buckeye butterfly as host plant

Rosemary (*Rosmarinus officinalis*). Late winter/spring (and, often, repeat bloom in fall) nectar flowers for pollinators

*Virgin's bower (*Clematis lingusticifolia*). Climbing vine, nectar flowers in early summer

Grasses

California fescue (*Festuca californica*), Idaho fescue (*F. idahoensis*), purple three-awn grass (*Aristida purpurea*), deergrass (*Muhlenbergia rigens*), foothill needlegrass (*Nassella lepida*), wild rye grass (*Leymus condensatus*)

Enhancing the Wildlife Value of Your Garden

While the Adler garden is an example of how wildlife habitat was created from bare ground, infinite variations on design and plant palette could be considered for a similar landscape. And it can all be done on a much smaller scale. Enhancing the wildlife value of an existing garden may be as simple as starting with a birdbath or adding a native tree or shrub in the fall or massing nectar flowers in a sunny location. Fruit-bearing vines, such as the California wild grape, not only feed birds but also link vertical layers as they grow, making them an excellent choice for sunny locations in small gardens. The trumpet creeper and honeysuckle vines are favorites of hummingbirds. Large pots of nectar flowers that bloom in different seasons will attract bees, butterflies, and other pollinators. Multifunctional plants that provide seed, nectar, pollen, nuts, or fruit in different seasons form the basis of a thriving wildlife sanctuary.

Just as important as the plants we choose, however, is the way we garden. The Adler garden embodies both concepts: a diversity of food and nectar plants combined with environmentally friendly gardening practices. A commitment to gardening organically not only benefits wildlife but also helps protect local watersheds—those large areas of land where rainwater, all too often laden with garden chemicals and other pollutants, makes its way to streams, rivers, lakes, bays, and, finally, to the ocean. Other sustainable practices, such as recycling all plant debris on site, minimizing lawn areas, and using permeable pathways to keep rainfall on the landscape, are wildlife-friendly practices that conserve water and energy.

Whether all-native habitat or a mix of native and other regionally appropriate plants, California wildlife gardens are environmentally friendly, easy to create and maintain, and affordable. They are daily invitations to observe and enjoy the beauty of birds, insects, and other creatures—and the plants that sustain them. The wildlife garden is a dynamic garden, evolving and changing through the seasons and through the years. It becomes a sanctuary not just for wildlife but for people, too—an opportunity to connect with Nature and to the drama, seen and unseen, that plays out each day on the backyard stage. Supporting this rich and diverse web of life generates multiple rewards, as you will discover in the chapters that follow.

A "bee block" in the Adler garden provides homes for cavity-nesting native bees.
PHOTOGRAPH BY MARYBETH KAMPMAN.

The Basics

Imitate Nature. Natural habitat has a layered look with a loose, natural design. Vertical, overlapping layers—from trees and shrubs to vines and ground plants—offer shelter, nesting, and foraging sites to birds, insects, and many other creatures. So do logs, dead trees, rock piles, and small brush piles. Repeating drifts of nectar flowers are especially attractive to butterflies and other pollinating insects.

Nature loves diversity. Imitate Nature by growing a wide variety of regionally appropriate food and nectar plants that bloom in different seasons. Consider fruit trees, berry bushes, an herb or food garden for seasonal produce. Excess fruit and seeds will feed birds and other wildlife; flowering fruit trees and herbs in the food garden offer nectar and pollen for bees and other pollinators. A mix of deciduous and evergreen trees and shrubs offers the most wildlife value in all seasons. Flowering vines make good use of vertical space, especially for small gardens.

Emphasize native plants. Native plants are the foundation of a wildlife garden; they have evolved with birds, insects, and other local wildlife in a complex web of life that is mutually nourishing. Natives are low-water-use plants, the ones best suited to our soils and climate.

Adopt an informal, less manicured look. Be less eager to prune and clip and clean up. A tidy, well-manicured garden is not a wildlife-friendly garden. Butterfly chrysalides may be found almost anywhere—on stems and branches, in brush piles or woodpiles, on windowsills or rocks.

Let trees and shrubs reach their normal size, flower, and set fruit; allow flowers and grasses to go to seed for birds and other creatures. Bare earth or soil that is lightly covered in leaf litter allows native bees to burrow into the ground to make their nests. The larvae of beetles also overwinter in the soil. Consider allowing at least part of your wildlife garden to be "wild."

Wildlife gardens are organic gardens. Wildlife gardens are easy to maintain, conserve water, and do not require synthetic fertilizers, pesticides, and herbicides. Recycle plant material as compost, leaf mulch, or small brush piles. Use permeable pathways and other eco-friendly practices whenever possible. Organic gardening is much more than not spraying plants with pesticides. Growing healthy soil, cultivating biodiversity, restoring and protecting watersheds—and providing habitat for wildlife—is the big picture of gardening organically.

All wildlife need water. Provide a regular source of clean, fresh water. Shallow containers of moist sand or soil provide moisture and minerals for butterflies. Water in ponds or containers attract toads and frogs.

An Umber Skipper nectars on catmint. Plants in the mint family are very attractive to butterflies and other pollinators. PHOTOGRAPH BY ROBERT WATKINS.

CHAPTER 2

Bird Habitat: From Quail to Hummingbirds

By planting natives and restoring "balance" and the circle of life in our own yard, we've taken a bird count of 50 species a year and turned it into 110-plus species. You build it and they will come.

— Ken Gilliland, bird habitat gardener

Many bird species feed on the edible fruit of blue elderberry (*Sambucus mexicana*). PHOTOGRAPH BY MIEKO WATKINS.

From the Red-tailed Hawk effortlessly riding the thermals to the male Anna's Hummingbird aggressively defending his territory, birds are the big players on the garden stage. Birds use all of the vertical layers of trees, shrubs, vines, and ground plants, and each species shows a preference for which layer is best for perching, foraging, and nesting. Raptors, for example, stay high in the tree canopy while quail, towhees, and juncos reside in the understory, where they feed on tender shoots, buds, and seeds or scrabble through the dust searching for insects. California Quail and other ground-nesters need dense cover or thickets for nesting, while cavity nesters, such as woodpeckers, bluebirds, and some owl species, look for holes in trees and snags. Back-

OPPOSITE: Spring-blooming pink-flowering current (*Ribes sanguineum*) is very attractive to hummingbirds. PHOTOGRAPH BY MARYBETH KAMPMAN.

33

The bright red berries of toyon (*Heteromeles arbutifolia*) in winter attract a House Finch (right) and Northern Mockingbird (below). PHOTOGRAPHS BY ROBERT WATKINS.

yard bird habitat imitates Nature by providing a diversity of plant shelters that meet the needs of various bird species for foraging and nesting sites.

The Specialists and the Omnivores

Any tree, shrub, vine, or ground plant that is good habitat for insects will provide food for 90 to 95 percent of the songbird species, and virtually all bird species need insects to feed their young.

Nectar-feeding orioles and hummingbirds also supplement their diet with insects. With its slender beak, the Black Phoebe skims insects off ponds and hawks for insects in the air, while Bushtits appear suddenly in flocks of a dozen or more, flit through the shrubbery, glean the insects, and move on just as quickly as they arrived. Finches and California Towhees, on the other hand, are primarily seed-eating species; goldfinches love sunflower seeds but they have also been seen shredding the leaves as well! Instead of feeding insects to their young, finches regurgitate partially digested seeds for their nestlings. Seed-eating birds have short, chunky beaks that are perfectly shaped for cracking open seeds. Many bird species, however, are omnivores: they eat insects *and* seeds, fruit, or nuts. Juncos, for example, eat mostly seeds in winter, but fill in with insects when seeds or fruit are not available. Some omnivores—Northern Mockingbirds, Cedar Waxwings, and American Robins, for example—love berries and other fruit.

Native berry-producing trees and shrubs, such as toyon, blue elderberry, hollyleaf cherry, and coffeeberry, feed many songbird species from summer into the winter months. Blue elderberry (*Sambucus mexicana*), with its beautiful form and large clusters of creamy white flowers,

The nectar-rich, fragrant blossoms of blue elderberry (*Sambucus mexicana*) attract pollinators and beneficial insects in late spring. PHOTOGRAPH BY MIEKO WATKINS.

makes a dramatic specimen plant or useful hedge or screen. The nectar-rich flowers in spring attract pollinators, and many songbirds love the tasty dark blue berries that follow as well as the insects this plant attracts. (The berries from the blue elderberry are edible and often used in jams and syrups.) Hollyleaf cherry and coffeeberry provide nectar flowers in spring and berries for birds in summer and fall; both attract beneficial insects looking for nectar, pollen, and insect prey. These berry-producing shrubs are better choices for the wildlife garden than non-native pyracantha or invasive privet and cotoneaster, which birds spread into wild lands by eating the fruit.

For a low-growing hedge or mounding ground cover, the handsome Oregon grape (*Berberis aquifolium*) with its glossy, holly-like leaves and yellow flowers in spring is an excellent choice. It is drought tolerant and easy to grow in most garden soils, it provides cover and foraging sites, and birds love its succulent berries. The more trees and shrubs you plant that produce seeds, nuts, berries, and fruit, the more bird species you'll attract to your bird habitat. By improving the carrying capacity of your habitat garden throughout the year with a diversity of available food sources, artificial feeding will not be necessary or, at the least, can be kept at a minimum. Because native trees and shrubs are such important sources of food and nectar, and because they support a high number of insects that birds feed on, they are an essential part of a wildlife garden that focuses on bird habitat.

This hedgerow of California lilac (*Ceanothus* spp.), coffeeberry (*Rhamnus californica* 'Eve Case'), and dwarf coyote bush (*Baccharis pilularis*) provides food, cover, and nesting sites for birds and beneficial insects.
PHOTOGRAPH BY PAT HUNT.

The Multifunctional Hedgerow

Hedgerows are welcome sights for winged wildlife, whether local birds or weary migrants looking for a safe rest stop or overwintering site. Fortunately, they are making a comeback in this country. A traditional feature of the English countryside, hedgerows were once common here, too, before they were relentlessly replaced with fences. Once again they are reappearing in orchards, vineyards, even suburban

TOP: Even in winter coffeeberry (*Rhamnus californica*) provides food for birds. PHOTOGRAPH BY PAT HUNT.

BOTTOM: Coyote bush (*Baccharis pilularis*) attracts many birds and beneficial insects. PHOTOGRAPH BY MIEKO WATKINS.

lots. You don't need to own a ranch to plant a beautiful and multi-functional hedgerow. Hedgerows are versatile enough to accommodate acreage of almost any size. They may simply mark a garden boundary or do double duty as a windbreak or privacy screen. Hedgerows stabilize soils and help the land retain moisture. While the hedgerow has many useful functions as part of the landscape, it moves beyond practicality in a wildlife garden.

Hedgerows have enormous wildlife value: they offer dense cover, a multitude of nesting sites, and a diversity of seasonal food sources. Songbirds flourish in the dense, multi-tiered structure and California Quail, California Towhees, and Dark-eyed Juncos forage and nest in the thick underbrush.

A hedgerow is a mixture of trees and/or flowering shrubs that typically includes an understory of grasses and nectar flowers. Unlike the meticulously clipped formal hedge, which is neat and uniform and unappealing to wildlife, hedgerow plants are allowed to flower, set fruit, and grow to their mature size. Consider several factors when choosing plants for a hedgerow—height and width desired, function in the landscape, and the local soil and climate. Tall trees such as willows, cottonwoods, box elder, and bay double as cover and windbreaks. Evergreen shrubs provide dense shelter, nesting, and foraging sites for birds and beneficial insects. Stagger bloom times within the mix of trees or shrubs to increase wildlife value year-round. For example, willows and manzanitas bloom in January and February; California lilac (*Ceanothus* spp.) from February through March; hollyleaf cherry (*Prunus ilicifolia*) and coffeeberry (*Rhamnus californica*) in April and May; Mexican elderberry and toyon (*Heteromeles arbutifolia*) from May to June; coyote bush (*Baccharis pilularis*) from October through December. Vary bloom times

of understory plants to offer wildlife additional nectar and pollen sources in all seasons.

Three native evergreen shrubs—coffeeberry, California lilac, and coyote bush—make an attractive combination with great wildlife value. All three shrubs bring in many kinds of insects, which, in turn, feed birds and the many beneficial insects—ladybird beetles, lacewings, hoverflies—these shrubs attract. Wax myrtle (*Myrica californica*), an evergreen native shrub, presents a more refined hedge for inland suburban gardens; it is especially suitable for coastal gardens. Its waxy nutlets are food for robins and finches. Dogwoods (*Cornus* spp.) have great wildlife value: over 20 species of birds use them for cover, nesting, and foraging. *Grevillea* 'Canberra', a non-native drought-tolerant evergreen shrub,

A hedge of *Grevillea* 'Canberra' provides cover for California Quail and the flowers feed hummingbirds, even in the winter.
PHOTOGRAPH BY PAT HUNT.

grows up to ten feet in height and blooms most of the year with nectar-rich flowers that hummingbirds love. The heaviest bloom is in winter, a time when food sources are scarce for Anna's Hummingbird, our year-round resident. The *Grevillea* species, hardy shrubs from Australia that can take heat and poor soils, are also attractive to other bird species for the seeds and the cover they provide.

Try to use locally sourced plants with similar needs for soil, sun, and water. Planting in the fall and winter to take advantage of the winter rainy season offers plants the best start. Know how big the plants will grow and make allowances. Depending on the desired outcome, shrubs could be spaced as close as four to six feet apart for a dense thicket. On roomier lots and for greater diversity consider combining a few canopy trees—bay laurel, oaks, California buckeye, for example—with a mix of evergreen shrubs. Because hedgerows can be created with many different heights, lengths and widths, they can be used as a living fence. Neighbors, for example, might plant double rows with different plants for each side of the "fence," multiplying cover, food, and nesting sites for birds and other wildlife. (See Appendix D: Plants for Hedgerows.)

Hummingbird Havens

The Ruby-throated Hummingbird makes yearly solo flights from the Yucatan Peninsula to the coast of Texas—600 miles nonstop across the Gulf of Mexico. The Rufous Hummingbird may travel from as far north as Alaska to spend winter in southern Mexico, a one-way trip of over 2,000 miles! These are impressive feats for a tiny creature barely four inches long and weighing no more than a quarter. Hummingbird acrobatics, including flying backwards, are no less amazing. As part of its mating ritual, the male Anna's Hummingbird skyrockets straight up into the sky, then suddenly plunges downward in a noisy kamikaze dive. These tiny birds are anything but timid, as any habitat gardener knows. Males aggressively defend their territory from larger birds, and especially from other male hummers. This fierce competitiveness is not surprising given the critical importance of their food sources. To support a very

fast metabolism and those high-speed chases, hummers need a constant source of nutrients. With their long tongues, they sip sucrose in the form of nectar from tubular shaped flowers, scooping up small insects as they feed or catching them on the fly. (Another reason not to use pesticides: they not only contaminate the nectar flowers, but also kill the insects hummingbirds feed on.)

Two hummingbirds that migrate to Mexico in the fall—the Rufous and Allen's Hummingbirds—may also visit California gardens. The orange back of the male Rufous

Hummingbird sage (*Salvia spathacea*) serves as both feeding station for hummers and mounding groundcover. PHOTOGRAPHS BY MIEKO WATKINS.

A female Anna's Hummingbird nectars on the blossoms of *Salvia chiapensis* (top); A male Anna's takes a brief rest (bottom).
PHOTOGRAPHS BY ROBERT WATKINS.

is easy to distinguish from the green back of the Allen's (both have a green crown), but the females and immature of both species look alike. Both hummers migrate to Mexico in autumn. The Rufous breeds the farthest north of any hummingbird — from the Pacific Northwest to southern Alaska. Anna's and Allen's Hummingbirds nest in areas along the Pacific Coast. Anna's Hummingbird, our year-round resident, is the one you are most likely to see in your garden. The male is dark green with a rosy head and throat, though the bright colors may sometimes look black, depending on the light. The female may wear a few iridescent feathers on her throat, but she is far less showy. The Anna's male claims a nectar-rich territory and defends it against other males. He is a promiscuous fellow with many mating partners, and once mating is over, the female is on her own. Unlike many male birds that help with at least some of the chores, the Anna's male abandons the female to build the nest, brood, and raise the nestlings alone.

Hummingbirds use spider webs as glue to hold the nest materials together and decorate the outside of the nest with lichen as camouflage to blend in with the foliage. With their long, thin beaks, hummers sip nectar from deep-throated flowers. While they feed, pollen gets stuck on their bill and head and, sometimes, on their throats. In this way they provide pollinating services for some flowers. Though hummers will nectar on flowers of many colors, red and orange tubular-shaped flowers indicate a good nectar source and catch their attention more quickly than others. The bright red flowers of various *Salvia* and *Penstemon* species or the red-orange spikes of the red hot poker plant (*Kniphofia* spp.), for example, are especially attractive. (Orioles, also nectar feeders, are particularly fond of the red hot poker plant.) Unlike butterflies, hummingbirds hover as they nectar; they don't need landing platforms.

Early-spring-blooming native trees and shrubs, such as willows, manzanitas, ceanothus, and the *Ribes* species (currants and gooseberries), are important nectar sources for Anna's Hummingbird, which nests as early as December. Pink-flowering currant (*Ribes sanguineum*) flowers as early as January; chaparral current (*R. malvaceum*) and the fuchsia-flowered gooseberry (*R. speciosum*) are excellent winter sources of nectar for hummers. Later, in May, hummers flock to the large creamy flower clusters of California buckeye. The small scarlet flowers of island bush snapdragon (*Galvezia speciosa*), a sprawling, drought-tolerant (but frost-tender) native evergreen shrub from the Channel Islands, bloom most of the year. Fast-growing native bladderpod (*Isomeris arborea*) also has a long bloom season; it's one of the best hummingbird shrubs for areas that experience mild winters. Consider a clematis, honeysuckle, or trum—pet vine for a fence or at the base of a snag; it will quickly become a feeding station for hummingbirds.

Sages (*Salvia* spp.), workhorses of the habitat garden, are a must for hummingbird habitat. Excellent nectar plants, salvias also have great

Purple sage (*Salvia leuco-phylla* 'Pt. Sal Spreader') and Brandegee sage (*S. brandegeei*) are a magnet for native bees and butterflies in early spring.
PHOTOGRAPH BY MIEKO WATKINS.

wildlife value for butterflies, bees, and other pollinators. They are plants with unique beauty and a most distinctive aromatic scent. The spicy-scented foliage of sage may be subtle or quite strong, almost medicinal in the case of clary sage (*Salvia sclarea*), that wonderful salvia for dry sunny places. Salvias are the perfect fit for our Mediterranean climate — not water guzzlers, not demanding, very satisfying to grow. They know few limits on size and shape, appearing in forms that are tall and graceful, bushy and dense, slender and upright, sometimes softly mounding. Each species serves up its inimitable tubular flowers in equally diverse ways, from delicate whorls or sprays to dramatic spikes. Salvias, in general, tend to be low-water-use sun lovers. There are exceptions. Bog sage (*S. uliginosa*) likes its feet soggy, can handle heavy clay soils, and does fine with less than full sun. Hummingbird sage (*S. spathacea*) takes sun or shade (though it prefers light shade) and accepts summer garden water or practically none. Nectar flowers that attract hummers contain their own brand of scent and sugar solution (sucrose, fructose, glucose, or a mix of all three), all packaged in colors and shapes that will entice

The Gottlieb Garden: A Creative Solution

The Gottliebs' bird sanctuary in Los Angeles, a one-acre lot on top of a canyon, began in 1990 as a water-conservation effort. Susan Gottlieb, a self-described gardening novice, discovered California native plants as she researched drought-tolerant options to replace the Algerian ivy and exotics that covered the hillsides around her home. To her delight, Susan quickly realized she could combine her new interest in birding with restoring native plant habitat. The changeover from ivy to native plants is an on-going project that the owners have tackled one section at a time. Motivated by her desire to keep her four cats and the wildlife safe, Susan designed a cat run made of redwood planks and wire that runs through the property, from rooftop to tree canopy to understory. Platforms on the roof offer the cats safe bird-watching opportunities and the cat run is accessed at three different cat doors leading from the house into the run. The cats enjoy the action and the birds can feast, bathe, and drink in peace and safety.

Cats and birds co-exist peacefully in Susan Gottlieb's wildlife habitat garden.
PHOTOGRAPH BY SUSAN GOTTLIEB.

hummingbirds to visit. Complete your hummingbird habitat with a water source—a misting spray in a birdbath or pond is highly attractive to hummers. (See Appendix E: Seasonal Plants for Hummingbirds.)

Garden Profile

Quail Hollow, Tujunga, Los Angeles County

Seeking to enhance their existing bird habitat and to create a "green buffer zone," Ken and Rhonda Gilliland bought two adjoining vacant lots in the summer of 2001. Their goal was to create a wildlife friendly sanctuary with plenty of cover, nesting areas, and natural food sources for birds. Their canyon setting, which is mostly dry "urban oak scrub," is near the San Gabriel Mountains, about 25 miles from downtown Los Angeles. Winter temperatures vary greatly, but the highs of summer range from 75 to 100 degrees, and sometimes higher. Motivated by the need to avoid huge outlays in soil amendments, fertilizers, and water usage, the Gillilands decided to plant natives. "Little did we know," says Rhonda Gilliland, "that it was the beginning of a new gardening obsession. We had to give up some of our old favorites, but we went to work finding new native favorites. It was not a difficult task; we immediately fell in love with our amazing native plants." Starting with an Internet search, the Gillilands found two valuable resources: Las Pilitas Nursery web site, and the Theodore Payne Foundation Nursery, where the majority of the plants were purchased. Though the Gillilands read through much of the extensive material on the Pilitas web site, in the end they ignored whatever potential problems their property presented and simply jumped in.

Drawing from various native plant communities, they matched plants with the different soils and sun/shade conditions on their combined landscapes. For example, fairy duster (*Calliandra*

californica) and desert willow (*Chilopsis linearis*), two shrubs that bloom in the fall with flowers particularly attractive to hummingbirds, were planted in the "desert" section, a sunny area with sandy soil. Over a dozen species of salvias, including numerous cultivars of Cleveland sage,

Brandegee sage, and black sage, grow in the heavier soils of the mostly sunny "scrub" or "chaparral" sections. Extensive plantings of manzanita, ceanothus, and currants (*Ribes* spp.) throughout the garden offer cover and foraging sites and nectar for hummers during late-winter and early-spring bloom times. Birds feast on the seeds of these native shrubs and the insects they attract. Many berry-producing shrubs, such as coffee-

berry, lemonade berry, thimbleberry, and Oregon grape, provide fruit in summer and fall as well as cover and foraging sites.

Planted throughout the various gardens are a hundred species of native bulbs, annuals, and perennials (including eight species of wild onion, over a dozen species of native lilies and California buckwheat, and over 20 native *Penstemon* species) that attract insects and provide

PRECEDING SPREAD: Layers of shrubs and perennials flank a garden path. At left: *Verbena lilicina, Penstemon centranthifolius, Sphaeralcea ambigua.* At right: California poppies, *Solanum xanti* and *S. wallacei, Gnaphalium canescens, Lupinus latifolius parshii.* LEFT: Drought-tolerant native shrubs, including *Salvia clevelandii* 'Allen Chickering', fairy duster (*Calliandra californica*), *Salvia mellifera* x *sonomensis* 'Dara's Choice', and Indian mallow (*Abutilon palmeri*), offer cover and foraging sites and nectar for hummingbirds. PHOTOGRAPHS BY KEN GILLILAND.

nectar, pollen, and seed for pollinators and birds. Numerous bunchgrasses offer additional seeds, as well as cover and foraging sites. None of the existing trees and shrubs with wildlife habitat value that were compatible with native plants was removed. Pepper trees, grevillea, and deodar cedar (favored by nuthatches, chickadees, and creepers) provide cover, food sources, and nesting areas. A wisteria vine not only provides cover near the stream where birds love to bathe, but it is also a valuable spring-blooming nectar plant for hummingbirds and bees. The trumpet-shaped flowers of cape honeysuckle (*Tecomaria capensis*) are favored by hummingbirds and the foliage provides dense cover for many bird species.

From spring through winter, hummingbirds nectar on the flowers of manzanita, island bush snapdragon, woolly blue curls, native honeysuckle, dudleya, chuparosa, and numerous others. Stands of the multi-functional Hooker's evening primrose, which is especially attractive to bumblebees, bloom in spring through summer. Later, voluminous amounts of seed capsules arrayed along the stalks open daily one at a time, offering months of foraging for finches and other seedeaters. Desert mallows, coyote mint, asters, tarweeds, and other composites provide copious amounts of seeds and foraging opportunities as well. Over 500 native trees, shrubs, vines, herbaceous plants, and grasses have restored this canyon habitat into prime bird habitat.

Wildlife focus: Active birders, the Gillilands have been thrilled with

In April drifts of monkeyflower (*Mimulus bifidus* 'Big Tujunga Orange'), San Clemente Island bush mallow (*Malacothamnus clementinus*), and penstemons (*Penstemon spectabilis, P. grinnellii*) provide nectar, seeds and cover; the insects they attract feed birds and other wildlife. PHOTOGRAPH BY KEN GILLILAND.

the bird species that frequent their habitat. Over 100 bird species have been counted, including four species of hawks, seven species of hummingbirds, ten species of warblers, seven species of woodpeckers, and three species of flycatchers. California Quail are numerous and Nuttall's Woodpeckers nest in the garden, as do Spotted Towhees, Bushtits, Bewick's Wrens, Mourning Doves, House Finches, and California Towhees. The Gillilands especially look forward to the songs of the

Garden Profile

White-crowned Sparrows that arrive in the fall and the Black-headed Grosbeaks that show up in the spring. Because many of the native shrubs and herbaceous plants double as butterfly host, nectar and pollen plants, local butterflies, bees, and other pollinators are supported throughout the seasons.

Special features: Three small ponds pump water to artificial streams and waterfalls that provide a water source for wildlife and a riparian element to this otherwise dry canyon landscape. Ken built the streams by hand and lined them with local rocks from their land. Each pond pump has a recycle valve that can be turned on at night or when the owners are on vacation. This valve directs the water back into the ponds, bypassing the streams and waterfalls where debris can occasionally block the flow of water. Stream and pond edges are lined with native ferns, rushes, grasses, and showy flowering plants, such as giant stream orchids, monkeyflowers (*Mimulus lewisii* and *M. cardinalis*) and columbine (*Aquilegia* spp.). Large perennials, such as canyon sunflower (*Venegasia carpesioides*), are planted near the stream for cover.

Plant installation: The Gillilands first removed weeds and invasive non-native plants, then designed and planted their habitat sanctuaries themselves. The original front-yard habitat was finished within two years

and the newly acquired lots evolved over an additional two-year period. They used mostly 1-gallon plants and discovered that all of these plants outpaced the growth of the 5- to 15-gallon plants they purchased within the first or second year. Plants were selected according to their sun and soil requirements, and for their compatibility with the remaining trees and shrubs. Most of the plants were bought at the nearby Theodore Payne Foundation Nursery; others came from Rancho Santa Ana Botanic Garden plant sales and native plant mail order stores. Eager to begin, the Gillilands started planting in the month of June, the worst

Bushtits (opposite page) have chosen the Santa Cruz Island ironwood (*Lyonothamnus floribundus*) for a nest site (left).

PHOTOGRAPH BY KEN GILLILAND.

time to plant native trees and shrubs. They lost the first of the manzanitas, for example, to fungal diseases by introducing water during their naturally dormant period. However, they were successful with all of the natives they planted later in October.

Gardening practices: Acknowledging that there are differing opinions on how to water native plants, Ken favors the "do your research" approach: figure out where the plants evolved and try to mimic those natural conditions. Some of their natives require little to no supplemental water; some are watered weekly or less frequently. Plants that require regular water are situated near the ponds or stream. Young trees and shrubs are given the occasional deep soak the first year or so. The owners water all plants that need supplemental water by hand to make sure that only the plants that need additional water receive it. During the summers, all necessary watering is done in the evenings to achieve a deeper soak. The owners have learned that native plants that look droopy during the day in the hottest months generally revive by evening. If not, some water may be needed. Because the owners live near a fire zone, they occasionally sprinkle the established chaparral sections, though these plants do not require supplemental water.

Leaf litter is left where it falls under the tree canopy. This natural mulch is beneficial to the native plants and to ground foragers such as the juncos and towhees. Leaves on walkways are swept up and distributed as mulch to other areas outside the tree line. Rock, used as mulch in the desert and coastal sage scrub plant areas, mimics the natural conditions of these plant communities. Light pruning is done as needed during the year, but most seed heads are left on the shrubs for the birds in early summer. The Gillilands let annuals go to seed, collect the seed, and then pull the remaining plant material to keep the garden looking relatively tidy. Several snags and dead branches on the property have been preserved for woodpeckers and other birds.

Favorite habitat plants: Ken is partial to the native berry species —*Berberis* (Oregon grape, barberries), *Fragaria* (native strawberry), *Ribes* (currants and gooseberry), *Rubus* (thimbleberry, western raspberry, native blackberry, salmonberry) —for their beautiful flowers and their habitat value for many different bird species. For Ken, the giant salt-bush (*Atriplex lentiformis*) is another standout in the landscape. The rust-colored flower plumes look dramatic in summer against the gray-green foliage and this dense 15 x 15-foot shrub provides a safe haven from predators for California Quail. Ken says the neighbors have named the saltbush "Quail Hall." Rhonda considers the live oaks as "the cornerstone species in their area" and the favored habitat of a very special bird, the Oak Titmouse. She loves the salvias, especially Cleveland sage for its beautiful and fragrant flowers. Used by hummers

California Quail forage on the ground and use dense shrubs and hedgerows for nesting sites and protection against predators.
PHOTOGRAPH BY CINDY LAMAR.

and butterflies by day, its evening visitor is the Sphinx moth (which looks very similar to a hummingbird). Rhonda cites the Channel Island species as particular favorites—Santa Cruz Island ironwood for its delicate and fragrant foliage and interesting bark; island snapdragon (*Galvezia speciosa*), a hummingbird favorite, for its "frequent bloom, ease, and cover value"; and tree ceanothus (*Ceanothus arboreus*) for "stunning seasonal bloom, quick growth, and tidy appearance." The many variations of the penstemon flowers and the mariposa lilies (*Calochortus* spp.), which Rhonda refers to as "jaw droppers," are also among her favorite habitat plants.

Rewards: "Many of us feel powerless to stop widespread destruction of the environment," says Ken, "but we can do something. We can plant native plants in our own yards; we can save the planet one garden at a time." "The birds," adds Rhonda, "have become our heartfelt connection to the earth." The Gillilands have taken their habitat gardening experience into the community by volunteering as instructors for "gardening with natives" classes at the Theodore Payne Foundation. They also joined the Foundation's annual native plant garden tour in the spring of 2010.

Quail Hollow: Partial List of Native Plants

Trees and Shrubs

Barberries (*Berberis aquifolium* 'Compacta' and 'Golden Abundance', *B. aquifolium repens, B. fremontii*)

Bladderpod (*Isomeris arborea*)

Blue elderberry (*Sambucus mexicana*)

Bush mallows (*Malacothamnus fasciculatus, M. clementinus*, and others)

California black walnut (*Juglans californica*)

California lilacs (*Ceanothus arboreus, C. cuneatus, C. gloriosus, C. griseus, C. thyrsiflorus, C. tomentosus*, and cultivars)

Coffeeberries (*Rhamnus californica* 'Eve Case', *R. californica* 'Mound San Bruno', *R. crocea, R. ilicifolia*)

Coyote bush (*Baccharis pilularis* 'Pigeon Point', *B. sarothroides*)

Currants and gooseberries (*Ribes aureum, R. californicum, R. indecorum, R. malvaceum, R. menziesii, R. speciosum, R. viburnifolium*)

Desert mallows (*Sphaeralcea ambigua, S.* ssp. *rosacea*)

Desert willow (*Chilopsis linearis*)

Dogwoods (*Cornus glabrata, C. stolonifera*)

Fairy dusters (*Calliandra californica, C. eriophylla*)

Hollyleaf cherry (*Prunus ilicifolia*)

Huckleberries (*Vaccinium ovatum, V. ovatum* 'Thunderbird')

Island bush poppy (*Dendromecon harfordii*)

Island snapdragons (*Galvezia speciosa, G. speciosa* 'Firecracker')

Lemonade berry (*Rhus integrifolia*)

Manzanitas (*Arctostaphylos densiflora* 'Austin Griffiths', *A. glandulosa, A. hookeri franciscana, A. hookeri* x *pajaroensis* 'Sunset'; *A. uva-ursi* 'Anchor Bay', 'Pacific Mist', 'Emerald Carpet', and others)

Mountain mahogany (*Cercocarpus betuloides*); Island mahogany (*C. montanus*)

Oaks (*Quercus agrifolia, Q. berberidifolia, Q. douglasii, Q. kelloggii, Q. lobata*)

Sages (*Salvia apiana, S. brandegeei, S. clevelandii, S. leucophylla* 'Pt. Sal'; *S. mellifera* 'Dara's Choice' and 'Mrs. Beard')

Saltbush (*Atriplex lentiformis* ssp. *breweri*)

Santa Cruz Island ironwood (*Lyonothamnus floribundus*)

Snowberry (*Symphoricarpos* spp.)

Thimbleberry, western raspberry, native blackberry (*Rubus parviflorus, R. leucodermis, R. ursinus*)

Toyons (*Heteromeles arbutifolia, H.* 'Davis Gold')

Tree mallow/island mallow (*Lavatera/Malva assurgentiflora*)

Woolly blue-curls (*Trichostema lanatum*)

Several artificial streams on the Gilliland property provide a source of water for birds and other wildlife.
PHOTOGRAPH BY KEN GILLILAND.

Perennials, Annuals, and Biennials

Buckwheats (*Eriogonum arborescens, E. cespitosum, E. cinereum, E. crocatum, E. douglasii, E. fasciculatum, E. grande rubescens, E. latifolium, E. umbellatum*)

California fuchsia (*Epilobium* spp.)

Canyon sunflower (*Venegasia carpesioides*)

Columbine (*Aquilegia* spp.)

Coyote mints (*Monardella villosa, M. purpurea, M. macrantha* 'Marian Sampson', and others)

Evening primrose (*Oenothera elata hookeri*)

Lobelias (*Lobelia cardinalis pseudosplendens, L. dunnii serrata*)

Lupines (*Lupinus albifrons, L. benthamii, L. arboreus*)

Monkeyflowers (*Mimulus aurantiacus, M. cardinalis, M. guttatus, M. longiflorus rutilus, M. puniceus*, and others)

Penstemon spp. (*P. centranthifolius, P. clevelandii, P. eatonii, P. heterodoxus, P. heterophyllus, P. lateus, P. palmeri*, and others)

Pitcher sages (*Lepechinia fragans, L. hastata*; also *L. calycina*, a local species)

Sages (*Salvia sonomensis* 'Bee's Bliss', *S. spathacea*)

San Diego honeysuckle (*Lonicera subspicata denudata*)

Wallflowers (*Erysimum capitatum, E. franciscanum crassifolium, E. menziesii*)

Yarrow (*Achillea millefolium*)

Grasses and Sedges

Deergrass (*Muhlenbergia rigens*); fescues (*Festuca californica, F. idahoensis, F. rubra, F. rubra* 'Molate'); June grass (*Koeleria macrantha*); purple three-awn grass (*Aristida purpurea*); giant wild rye (*Leymus* 'Canyon Prince'); needlegrass species (*Nassella cernua, N. lepida, N. pulchra*); foothill sedge (*Carex tumulicola*), showy sedge (*C. spectabilis*), field sedge (*C. praegracilis*), globe sedge (*C. globosa*), Santa Barbara sedge (*C. barbarae*), big-leaf sedge (*C. amplifolia*)

Growing Bird Habitat

In creating Quail Hollow, the Gillilands made the decision to focus on diversity rather than design. Their wildly successful "demonstration garden" incorporates all of the basic needs of wildlife—food, cover, water—with an emphasis on providing plentiful nesting and foraging sites for birds. Evergreen and deciduous trees and shrubs of varying heights mix with herbaceous plants, grasses, and other groundcovers that serve as overlapping understory layers. Multiple layers of plants provide nourishment in the form of fruit, seeds, nuts, nectar, and pollen; the many insects these plants attract also feed birds and their young. Leaf litter, allowed to accumulate naturally, adds foraging options for bird species that look for seeds and insects on the ground. Nesting boxes, snags, and other deadwood offer additional nesting sites. Abundant water sources and the sound of moving water draw in local and migrant bird species, which find shelter and food as well. Before they bought plants for their wildlife sanctuary, the Gillilands followed some important steps.

Let the composites (aster-sunflower family) go to seed in the fall for the White-crowned Sparrows and other bird species.
PHOTOGRAPH BY SUSAN GOTTLIEB.

- First, they evaluated their site. They inventoried the plants that already existed on the land, looking for existing native plant communities and determining which non-native plants had wildlife value.
- Next, they researched the types of plants that would not only offer the best wildlife value for bird species, but would also have low water needs and be the most adaptable plants for their microclimate and soils. Then they matched the plants to the land's varying soil conditions and the plants' requirements for sun, shade,

and water. As much as possible, they made an effort to group plants from the same plant community (i.e., desert, chaparral, riparian) or with other plants with similar needs.

- They used local native plant nurseries for plant stock and they quickly learned that fall was an optimum time to plant natives, especially those with an aversion to summer water. Fall and winter planting gives natives time to grow the deep roots that allow them to get through the summer dry season.

- By doing their research carefully, the Gillilands learned where the plants they most wanted naturally grew and if they were adaptable to the conditions on their site. Because they have made the effort to put the right plant in the right place and because they recognize that native plants have different needs for sun, shade, and water, they have been rewarded with healthy plants and a thriving garden.

Bird Nest Boxes

Installing nest boxes in your garden is one way to extend bird cover and nesting options. Raptors and many songbirds, in particular, often have difficulty finding good nesting sites. Be sure that your nest box fits the special needs of whichever bird species you're trying to attract. Recycled untreated wood, especially redwood and cedar, is highly recommended. Pine and plywood, for example, would have to be painted on the outside for durability; however, the inside of a nest box should never be painted. Information on how to build nest boxes is readily available through bird conservation groups and other organizations. (See Appendix J, Books and Resources.) Wade Belew, a Sonoma County bird enthusiast and educator, has been building nest boxes for over 15 years. He offers the following caveats and tips.

- Many commercial "birdhouses" are disproportioned and the

entrance hole is too large. A standard nesting box should be twice as tall as it is wide. When the hole is too large, it is not safe for songbirds as more aggressive bird species may enter and drive them from the box.

- Most songbirds fit into a 1 1/2-inch entrance hole; smaller songbirds such as titmice, chickadees and nuthatches require a 1 1/4-inch entrance hole. A slightly larger hole, 1 9/16, for example, allows European Starlings to enter the box. If they get in, they will peck eggs and kill the nestlings. Three-inch holes are recommended for American Kestrels and Screech Owls and their nesting boxes should be placed at least 10 feet off the ground. Barn Owl boxes require 6-inch holes, 12-20 feet off the ground.

- Nest boxes should not have perches. Birds don't need them and they obstruct entry. Worse, they make the box more accessible to non-native bird species such as English House Sparrows, which may not only drive songbirds from their nests boxes but also kill the young.

- A nesting box should have an overhanging roof above the entrance and several 3/8-inch ventilation holes underneath the roof line (more holes are needed for a hot site) and three or four 3/8-inch drainage holes in the bottom of the box.

- A door that opens (on the top or side of the box) allows monitoring and cleaning of the box once a year after the breeding season is over.

- Avoid placing the box on a tree with lateral branches nearby, which allow raccoons and other predators easy access. Free-standing poles are another option.

Western Bluebirds and other songbirds face a shortage of nesting sites. Nest boxes with just the right-sized entrance hole are a welcome sight.
PHOTOGRAPH BY ROBERT WATKINS.

Enhancing Bird Habitat Value

There are many ways to enhance the bird habitat value of existing backyard (and frontyard) gardens. Add small shrubs, herbaceous plants, grasses, or other ground cover to increase understory layers beneath trees and large shrubs. Prostrate forms of valuable wildlife shrubs such as manzanitas and ceanothus provide attractive groundcovers for slopes and dense shelter for birds. Consider a hedgerow or flowering hedge as habitat, boundary screen, or windbreak. If space is at a premium, look for places to add vines — fence, trellis, or garden shed — that offer nectar

flowers in spring or fruit in the fall. When it's time to replace a shrub, choose a berry-producing native shrub, such as coffeeberry, hollyleaf cherry, or blue elderberry. Choose hummingbird plants that will flower in each season or that have long bloom periods. Plant sunflowers, asters, and other composites—they are good companions for vegetable gardens—and remember to let them go to seed in the fall for finches and other seedeaters. Fresh water in a birdbath or re-circulating fountain is a welcome sight for birds while providing hours of viewing pleasure. If there is a creek on your property, consider restoring wildlife habitat by replacing any invasive non-native plants with elderberry species, dogwoods, willows, sedges, and other native riparian plants. Depending on the region, only 2-14 percent of California's historical riparian habitat remains. It is considered crucial habitat for dozens of local birds and overwintering migrants. (For plant suggestions for riparian areas, see Appendix B: Native Plant Communities and Appendix D: Plants for Hedgerows.)

Bird Habitat Basics

Layer your landscape with a mix of trees, shrubs, herbaceous plants, and grasses. Plant as many native plants as possible, especially berry-producing trees and shrubs. Because nesting sites are at a premium for the cavity nesters, try to leave as much deadwood as possible when pruning unless it's a fire hazard or too close to structures. Avoid cutting trees or pruning shrubs during the songbirds' nesting season, which generally lasts from mid-March through August in California.

Let your flowers, especially the composites (sunflower family), go to seed in the fall. They will feed finches, juncos, and other seed-eating birds from fall into winter. Don't be so quick to tidy up. When you clean up the garden in the autumn, you are cleaning up the supply of insects and seeds that birds depend on to get through the winter.

California poppies, tansyleaf phacelia (*Phacelia tanacetifolia*), bladderpod (*Isomeris arborea*), bush anemone (*Carpenteria californica*), and purple sage (*Salvia sonomensis* 'Bee's Bliss') provide cover and food for birds and insects. PHOTOGRAPH BY KEN GILLILAND.

ABOVE: A Hermit Thrush forages for insects among plant debris on the ground. FACING PAGE: The Gillilands' bird habitat offers many vertical plant layers—from canopy to grasses—that provide food, cover, nesting, and foraging sites. PHOTOGRAPHS BY KEN GILLILAND.

Provide a source of fresh water for drinking and bathing year-round. Keep birdbaths clean and filled with fresh water. Be sure to scrub out regularly with a brush and biodegradable dish detergent as needed. Protect watering stations from predators. Place birdbaths near cover but far enough away from shrubbery to prevent surprise attacks from cats. Whenever possible, keep cats out of habitat areas, especially during nesting season. Both feral and well-fed domestic cats are avid and skilled hunters. Where there is cat predation, bird numbers go down. Research shows that bells on collars do not work.

Leave some leaf litter on the ground. Birds forage for insects and seeds in leaf litter and mulched flowerbeds and pathways. Provide logs and small brush piles for foraging sites.

If you use bird feeders, be sure to keep them clean. Bird feeders can spread disease among wild bird populations from contaminated food, water, and feeder surfaces. Most bird conservation organizations recommend feeders that exclude songbird predators such as jays and crows. If you use hummingbird feeders, be sure to wash them thoroughly at each refill. If you go on vacation and feeders will not be maintained, it's better to take them down rather than risk infecting your local hummingbirds.

Please don't use insecticides, herbicides, and other poisons. Make your garden a safe sanctuary for wildlife. Rodenticides harm owls, hawks, and other raptors, which die from accidental secondary poisoning when they eat rodents killed by products containing the anti-coagulant brodifacoum. See www.hungryowl.org for more information on this subject.

CHAPTER 3

The Pollinator Garden: Butterflies, Bees, and Other Beneficial Insects

I don't need to travel the world; I am deeply rooted in California and perfectly content nurturing my garden. Each day I see something new, some small thing that brings insight into the larger ecosystem that surrounds me and that provides for so many creatures.

—Charlotte Torgovitsky, wildlife habitat gardener

The butterfly, a symbol of beauty in any language, is a miracle of transformation, as anyone who has witnessed the cycle of egg to caterpillar to chrysalis to emerging butterfly can attest. The ephemeral beauty of butterflies gives them unique status in the insect world; they are one kind of insect that virtually everyone is delighted to see in their garden. However, many butterfly species are suffering significant population declines; some species are facing extinction. Widespread use of pesticides and herbicides, butterfly collecting, and global warming may all contribute to butterfly population declines. However, the single cause that almost everyone can agree on is the destruction of natural habitat. What ensues from the destruction of habitat is the disappearance of plants that are essential for butterfly reproduction.

While butterflies can feed on many different nectar plants, butterfly caterpillars require specific host plants. Without a bountiful supply of

The Anise Swallowtail butterfly uses umbellifers as caterpillar food plants. PHOTOGRAPH BY ROBERT WATKINS.

FACING PAGE: In Charlotte's front border (see Garden Profile, p. 96) pitcher sage (*Lepechinia hastata*) provides nectar for pollinators. PHOTOGRAPH BY MIEKO WATKINS.

67

the necessary host plants, breeding populations of each butterfly species becomes imperiled. While we cannot duplicate native ecosystems in our backyards, each wildlife garden makes a difference in providing habitat that butterflies otherwise have lost to human development. Planting for butterflies is an easy way to begin. If you plant for butterflies, other plant pollinators (and beneficial insect predators) will surely follow.

Plant for Butterfly Caterpillars

Adult butterflies live, on average, for three weeks and in that short period of time, they have a major and essential job to do: to mate and reproduce. The female butterfly must search for the appropriate larval food plants on which to lay her eggs, often limited to members of one or several plant families. Butterfly caterpillars are specialists; approximately 80 percent of butterfly larvae use only one plant family as host plants. Though host plants may be trees, shrubs, herbaceous plants, and grasses, butterfly caterpillars are host-specific; they do not munch their way through the garden eating everything in sight, a not uncommon misconception that makes some gardeners welcome adult butterflies but not their caterpillars. While a garden without caterpillar host plants may be a good place for butterflies to catch a quick sip of nectar, it cannot be considered habitat for butterfly reproduction.

A Painted Lady butterfly lays an egg on one of its host plants, chaparral mallow (*Malacothamnus fasciculatus*).
PHOTOGRAPH BY HARMINA MANSUR.

All native butterflies found here in California evolved with the local native plants as host plants, and for some butterfly species—the Pipevine Swallowtail and the California Sister, for example—there are no other options. Native trees and shrubs such as oaks, willows, and wild lilac (*Ceanothus* spp.) are primary caterpillar food plants for some of our most common California butterflies. Some butterfly species have adapted to non-native plants that are in the same plant family as the original host plant. For example, the Anise Swallowtail's primary native host plants were yampah (*Perideridia kelloggii*) and other members of the carrot family (Apiaceae). When wild fennel

(*Foeniculum vulgare*), also a carrot family member, arrived with the early European settlers, it quickly spread throughout California and soon became a favored host plant for the Anise Swallowtail butterfly. However, wild fennel is an invasive plant and not recommended for gardens. Other members of the carrot family, such as cow parsnip, culinary and bronze fennel, parsley, dill, lovage and angelica, are also used by the Anise Swallowtail as host plants for their eggs and caterpillars.

Because host plants for the Cabbage White butterfly (introduced to North America in the mid-1800s) are members of the mustard family, this butterfly may choose cabbage or other crucifers in your vegetable garden. Plant nasturtium, also a host plant for the Cabbage White, near your vegetable garden as a decoy. Weeds, or naturalized exotic plants, that are often found in rural areas along roadsides or in fields and pastures, and, sometimes, in urban gardens, have been adopted by various butterfly species as host plants. Though they may be problematic or invasive, many of them are valuable resources for some insects and birds. Wild mustard is a butterfly host plant for the Sara Orangetip, vetch and other pea family members serve the Silvery Blue butterfly, and the ubiquitous cheeseweed from the mallow family is an important host plant for the West Coast Lady, Painted Lady, and Common-checkered Skipper butterflies. Native host plants in the mallow family, such as checkerbloom (*Sidalcea malviflora*), a perennial wildflower, or the beautiful island mallow (*Lavatera assurgentiflora*), which are both easy to grow, are simply not as available to these butterfly species as the common cheeseweed.

Another weed, English plantain, is widely used by the Common Buckeye butterfly, in addition to several common garden plants. This handsome brown butterfly with orange markings and large eyespots uses some members of the snapdragon family as host plants. One gardener I know was horrified to find out that the dark caterpillars in her snapdragons, which she had meticulously picked off, were not insect pests but caterpillars of the Buckeye butterfly. She quickly resolved to

Monarch butterflies use only milkweed species as caterpillar food plants. Pictured here is narrow-leaf milkweed (*Asclepias fascicularis*). PHOTOGRAPH BY HARMINA MANSUR.

TOP: Passion vine is the only caterpillar food plant for the Gulf Fritillary. PHOTOGRAPH BY BOB STEWART. BOTTOM: A Gulf Fritillary nectars on Mexican sunflower (*Tithonia rotundifolia*). PHOTOGRAPH BY DONNA GRUBISIC.

plant more snapdragons and invest in a caterpillar guide! Both the Pipevine Swallowtail (northern California) and the Gulf Fritillary (coastal areas from the San Francisco area to southern California) have only one caterpillar host plant. The Pipevine Swallowtail, a large black butterfly with a metallic blue tint, uses only California pipevine (*Aristolochia californica*), which is most commonly found in riparian areas in northern California. If you are lucky enough to live where pipevine grows, consider planting two or three vines under a tree or on a trellis. Pipevine is found in moist shady places, often winding its way up trees or shrubs near streams or other damp areas or spreading out toward the sun from the base of a tree trunk. Though slow to start, once this vine takes off, generally in the second or third year, it will grow rapidly. The unusual pipe-shaped flowers appear before the bright green heart-shaped leaves; with a little luck, the handsome black and red caterpillars of the Pipevine Swallowtail will follow. If you live along the California coast where it is warm enough to grow the beautiful passion vine, you may entice the dark orange Gulf Fritillary into your garden. Passion vine, this tropical butterfly's only host plant, is a vigorous vine with striking lavender flowers. (*Note: Passiflora caerulea* is more caterpillar friendly than *P. alatocaerula*.)

Smaller host plants, such as perennials, should be planted in groups of at least three or more, preferably with several groups scattered around the garden, which may increase the larvae's odds against predators and parasitic insects. Though smaller plants and vines may look tattered if caterpillars have fed on them, they do revive, fertilized by caterpillar droppings called *frass*. Try to place host plants near nectar flowers, away from paths and borders, in sheltered areas of the garden where there is less noise, wind and foot traffic. Before planting new caterpillar host plants, check to see what plants butterflies may already be using on your land. Butterfly guides, county naturalists and some native plant nursery websites are easily available resources for finding out which butterflies are common in your area. (See Appendix F, Common California Butterflies and Host Plants.)

Caterpillar Defenses and Mimicry

The female butterfly searches for a host plant, testing prospective plants with her feet to take a reading of each plant's chemical composition. If the biochemicals in the plant are the right ones, she lays her eggs on the host plant, singly or in batches, with a glue-like substance. When a butterfly caterpillar emerges, it eats and grows, shedding its skin periodically, then eats and grows some more until it is ready to pupate, the next stage in its life cycle. At that point, butterfly caterpillars generally crawl away from the host plant and attach to twigs, branches, or stems of another plant. Most caterpillars hang upside down as they shed their skin and transform into a chrysalis, or pupa. Swallowtail caterpillars, however, affixed with a silken girdle at their abdomen, are

Monarch caterpillars feed on milkweed (*Asclepias curassavica*) at this Monarch Waystation in Santa Barbara. PHOTOGRAPH BY DONNA GRUBISIC.

mounted head up. Within the chrysalis the caterpillar undergoes a complete transformation, emerging as an adult butterfly several weeks or several months later, or, if the chrysalis has overwintered, it may not emerge for another year or more. At any stage of the life cycle, a butterfly species can go into hibernation, or *diapause*, for months or longer until conditions are more favorable. At which stage a butterfly

species enters diapause is predetermined: checkerspots always hibernate as caterpillars, for example; swallowtails, in the pupal stage. When adult butterflies emerge, they seek mates and look for nectar plants;

the females begin their search for a host plant and the cycle begins again.

Who cannot love the ephemeral beauty of butterflies or the little miracle of Nature they represent? Though perhaps not as beautiful, butterfly caterpillars, too, are fascinating creatures. They can spin silk and create a shelter in a leaf or form a drop line to the ground for a quick escape. Though they have many predators, butterfly caterpillars have an array of defenses. The Western Tiger Swallowtail caterpillar has large fake yellow eyes that may alarm a potential predator. Anise Swallowtail caterpillars display bright orange "horns," called *osmateria*, when frightened. They have a strong odor and resemble a snake's tongue, both of which may discourage a bird or other predator from attacking. The "Ladies"—American Lady, Painted Lady, and West Coast Lady butterfly caterpillars—wrap themselves in a leaf, held together with silken threads, as a protective covering against predators and parasitoids. Often colored in shades of green, brown and gray, caterpillars also use camouflage to blend with foliage, stems, and bark. The caterpillar of the Lorquin's Admiral has a unique brand of camouflage: its splotchy white-and-gray body looks just like bird droppings!

Monarch, Queen, and Pipevine Swallowtail butterfly caterpillars ingest toxic chemicals from their host plants that are passed on to the adult butterflies, making both caterpillar and adult distasteful, or poisonous, to birds. Birds learn to recognize by color and patterning which butterflies fall into that category. Some butterfly species that are not poisonous to birds use mimicry to fool their predators. The Viceroy butterfly, which resembles the Monarch's bright black-and-orange coloring, reaps the benefits of this warning pattern: birds are unable to distinguish one from the other. Other butterflies also use camouflage. The Mourning Cloak, a large chocolate-brown butterfly edged in a light-yellow ruffle, may live up to ten months hiding in tree crevices as an adult. With wings folded, its color and patterning make a good camou-flage against the bark. On warm winter days, this butterfly may appear from its hiding place to bask in the sun.

Swallowtail butterflies use the "tails" at the hind wing to draw a bird's attention to that part of the body, rather than the head. A bite out of the tail or hind wing may not prove to be fatal, but one from the head most certainly will. The large eyespots above the tails serve the same purpose; it's not uncommon to see swallowtails flying with tattered tails and wing edges. The black-and-white tipped "tails" of the Gray Hairstreak show large orange eyespots underneath. When this butterfly sips nectar, it moves the "tails" continuously to draw attention to that part of its body.

Each stage of metamorphosis—egg, caterpillar, pupa, adult—is vulnerable to predation from spiders, birds, and predatory insects. Parasitoids, parasitic wasps and flies that lay their eggs on or within the butterfly caterpillars, are a further threat. The fly or wasp larvae slowly feed on the living caterpillar, eating the least important organs first. Usually the caterpillar pupates and the parasitoids, which have pupated inside the caterpillar, emerge as adults. The odds that a butterfly cycle will be completed are not favorable. If just one or two butterflies emerge from a hundred—or even two hundred—eggs, it is considered a good survival rate!

Butterfly Nectar Plants and Nutrient Sources

Butterflies are nectar feeders, but they also may take in nutrients from damp soil or sand, from rotting fruit, animal droppings, and carrion. If you are lucky enough to have a butterfly land on you, it is most likely looking for moisture and minerals from your salty perspiration. Butterflies, which sip nectar through a long tubular mouthpart called a *proboscis*, search for flowers with easily accessible nectaries. The open faces of the composites,

Milkweed species double as butterfly nectar and caterpillar food plants. Pictured here is showy milkweed (*Asclepias speciosa*). PHOTOGRAPH BY MIEKO WATKINS.

members of the sunflower family (Asteraceae), fit the butterfly's needs perfectly. Members of this large plant family—asters, sunflowers, coreopsis, zinnias, daisies, coneflowers, and many others—have numerous and easily accessible nectaries in a single flower disk. They also offer broad landing pads and a long bloom season.

Native trees and shrubs—California buckeyes, ceanothus, bush mallows, for example—are good sources of nectar in early spring;

perennial and annual wildflowers from spring through fall. California buckwheat species, milkweed, California brittlebush (*Encelia californica*), coyote mint (*Monardella villosa*), California aster (*Aster chilensis*), goldenrod (*Solidago* spp.) and numerous other native perennials attract many butterfly species from summer into late fall. The fragrant panicles of butterfly bush (*Buddleia* spp.) and the tiny clusters of flowers on lantana and verbenas, for example, are very enticing to butterflies; many butterfly gardeners rank *Verbena bonariensis* at the top of their nectar plant lists. Mexican sunflower (*Tithonia rotundifolia*) and old-fashioned zinnias are highly attractive to Monarchs and other butterflies in late summer and fall. (See Appendix G, Top Nectar and Pollen Plant Families.)

Butterfly Habitat

How a gardener gardens impacts the butterfly at all stages of its life cycle. If the garden is kept clipped, tidy, and manicured, butterflies will have a much more difficult time reproducing, even if there are multiple food and nectar plants. Eggs, caterpillars, and chrysalides hide in the shrubbery on leaves, twigs, and stems. They need places to live over the winter—leaf litter, even brush piles—at all stages of their life cycle. A good strategy is to identify all caterpillar food plants in the garden. Because a host plant may look ragged while caterpillars are feeding, it might easily be pulled, trimmed or cut—a bad idea for the larvae. If a host plant is accidentally pruned, tuck the trimmings under the plant to insure a better chance of survival for larvae that may be on them.

Sheltered, sunny areas with drifts of nectar flowers, flowering trees, shrubs that bloom in different seasons, and caterpillar host plants provide attractive habitat for butterflies. Butterflies seek moisture rather than a water source. A shallow saucer filled with moist pebbles or sand serves as a good watering hole for butterflies and other insects. Male butterflies gather at muddy puddles and at the shallow edges of ponds

OPPPOSITE: For many butterfly gardeners *Verbena bonariensis* tops the list of good butterfly nectar plants and is very effective when massed.
PHOTOGRAPH BY MIEKO WATKINS.

BELOW: An American Lady, still able to fly with a bite out of its wings, nectars on coyote mint.
PHOTOGRAPH BY MIEKO WATKINS.

where they ingest minerals and other nutrients from the wet soil. Perhaps most important of all — be an organic gardener! Butterflies are extremely sensitive to chemicals; even the pesticide alternative Bt (*Bacillus thuringiensis*) is especially fatal to butterfly caterpillars.

Monarch Waystations

Each fall, Monarch butterflies in North America begin their migration southward from Canada to overwintering sites in Mexico and California thousands of miles away (Monarch populations east of the Continental Divide *generally* migrate to Mexico; west of the Divide, *generally* to coastal sites in California). California Monarchs mate in late winter, leave their overwintering sites, and begin their journey northward, searching for milkweed species where the females lay eggs and then die. Three or four successive generations breed from spring through late fall, but it is the last generation of Monarchs that fly to overwintering sites along the California coast, often floating on thermals to conserve energy. Summer generations of Monarchs live from four to six weeks; the last generation can live up to eight months.

These well-loved and most easily recognized butterflies are in such serious decline that in 2010 the World Wildlife Fund listed Monarchs, for the first time, as one of the ten most threatened species. Monarchs are losing habitat, and their host plants along roadsides and in croplands are disappearing due to the widespread use of herbicides. Fields of genetically modified corn and soybeans have also severely affected milkweed

CROSSOVER: Layers of shrubs and perennials in this front border (see Garden Profile, p. 96) provide nectar and pollen all year round.
PHOTOGRAPH BY MIEKO WATKINS.

BELOW: A Painted Lady nectars on coneflower (*Echinacea purpurea*).
PHOTOGRAPH BY CINDY LAMAR.

species, many of which grow on agricultural lands. "The planting of these crops genetically modified to resist the non-selective systemic

herbicide glyphosate," reports Monarch Watch, a program based at the University of Kansas, "allows growers to spray fields with this herbicide instead of tilling to control weeds." The Monarch Waystation program sponsored by the University of Kansas seeks to help alleviate the obstacles that Monarchs now face. Through this program home gardeners, schools, and community organizations have joined together to create "waystations" along the Monarch's migratory route that provide milkweed, nectar plants, and shelter to migrating Monarchs. (See the Blackstone Monarch Habitat in Ch. 5.)

Easy-to-grow tropical milkweed (*Asclepias curassavica*) overwinters in frost-free areas of California. PHOTOGRAPH BY BOB STEWART.

Donna Grubisic faces a different but persistent obstacle at her certified Monarch Waystation in Santa Barbara: the tachinid fly. Often called "the bane of the Monarch," tachinid flies lay their eggs on butterfly caterpillars. Used by local farmers as a biological control against caterpillars, this beneficial insect is not particular about which caterpillars it lays its eggs on. Monarch caterpillars, of course, are not the target; they feed only on the milkweed that grows on the land. Unfortunately, the flies have moved beyond the nearby croplands to city gardens and many butterfly species are under siege. Though Monarchs and Gulf Fritillaries, which also breed at this Waystation, suffer from the fly, they are, fortunately, less severely affected when summers are cool and foggy.

From over 100 native milkweed species in North America, twelve are native to California. Mixing different species in the garden is ideal, but always grow at least three plants of each species you choose. Native milkweeds die back in the winter and foliage emerges rather late in spring. Be sure to mark their location to avoid accidentally digging them up or losing them to more aggressive neighboring plants. Look for milkweed at native plant nurseries, plant sales at botanical gardens and garden clubs, and seed companies. The following milkweed species are easy to grow and are generally the most readily available. All need a sunny site, water to get established, and good drainage. *Note:* Oleander aphids are commonly found on milkweed species. They do not "jump" to other plants and may attract beneficial insects, such as ladybird beetles, lacewings, and hoverflies. Their larvae will soon make short work of the aphids. If you have waited patiently and aphids have covered the plant, a spray of eco-friendly dish detergent and water will wash them off. Please check first for caterpillars!

Showy milkweed (*Asclepias speciosa*) has large leaves and pink-tinged flowers.
PHOTOGRAPH BY HARMINA MANSUR.

- Narrowleaf milkweed (*Asclepias fascicularis*). White flowers with slender stems and foliage, 2-4 feet tall, hardy perennial, and drought tolerant. The most adaptable native milkweed for gardens, it is widespread throughout California and an especially good choice for coastal areas.
- Showy milkweed (*A. speciosa*). Pink-and-white, large, fragrant flowers and thick leaves, 3–5 feet tall, needs water in the early growing stages. This native milkweed may be slow to get established.
- Indian milkweed (*A. eriocarpa*). Pale yellow flowers tinged in pink, 3-4 feet tall, hardy perennial and drought tolerant; a California native.
- Tropical milkweed (*A. curassavica*). Red-and-yellow flowers; *A. curassavica* 'Silky Gold' has yellow flowers. Native to Mexico and South America, this milkweed needs regular water, is easy

to grow in pots, and is easy to propagate. A tender perennial, it will overwinter in frost-free areas and blooms all year round in some areas of southern California. In most areas of northern California, however, it is grown as an annual. Monarch caterpillars will feed on this milkweed, even if they have already started feeding on a different species. *A. curassavica* tests very high in cardiac glycocides, the chemicals in milkweed that give Monarchs protection against predators.

- *A. linaria* and *A. subulata* are desert species that may also attract the Queen butterfly, which also uses milkweed species as host plants, and is generally found in the desert regions of California.
- Swamp milkweed (*A. incarnata*) and common milkweed (*A. syriaca*), two milkweed species native to the East Coast, are suitable for moist sites. Both are typically available through seed catalogs.

Many scientists and butterfly advocates warn against the practice of releasing Monarchs, and other butterflies, at events. This lucrative business, hard to justify on humane grounds, could negatively impact native butterfly populations. The butterflies that survive the process of being released in this fashion may be unable to feed or breed in non-native habitat, or at the wrong season. Infected butterflies could spread disease to native populations, and there is concern that interbreeding among captive and native populations could lead to genetic alterations that may affect migratory behavior as well as other aspects of their life cycles. "Introducing large numbers of captive raised insects into the wild raises concerns for the spread of pathogens," reports Sonia Altizer, professor at the University of Georgia, and researcher Jaap de Roode (*American Butterflies*, Summer 2010), "because rearing animals at high densities in commercial operations could increase their exposure to some diseases." Currently, butterflies raised in commercial butterfly farms are not required by the USDA to be screened for parasites. At a time when our wild populations of many butterfly species are threatened, it seems a risk not worth taking.

Bees Are the Stars

Eighty percent of our food plants worldwide are pollinated primarily by insects. Butterflies, moths, wasps, flies—even some beetle species—are pollinators, but bees, of course, are the stars. Unlike other pollinators, bees deliberately collect pollen as food for their larvae. Over 100 crops in this country are bee-pollinated and the honeybee carries a considerable part of that load. Honeybees are not native bees but were brought here from Europe, most likely in the 1600s. They have, however, been in severe decline for several decades from various causes and afflictions—mites, fungal parasites, pesticides, and most recently, colony collapse disorder—that have devastated honeybee populations.

A honeybee nectars on purple sage (*Salvia leucophylla* 'Pt. Sal'). PHOTOGRAPH BY MIEKO WATKINS.

There is reason to believe that the issue is more complex than the afflictions themselves. Some entomologists point to the practice of hauling hives long distances from orchard to orchard just before trees flower. The stress of these long journeys—combined with pesticide exposure—may impair the bees' immune systems, making them more vulnerable to viruses and other infections. Other experts are concerned that bees become weakened by feeding on only one type of pollen, an orchard of almonds, for example, and are suffering from malnutrition. The plants that honeybees forage on provide the food they need to keep their colonies healthy, and many different types of pollens provide an extensive array of nutrients, all necessary for bee health. One single pollen source may not meet those nutritional needs. Beekeepers have treated bees with antibiotics to kill mites; as a result, a new strain of drug-resistant super mites has appeared, another contribution to the honeybees' demise. Though native bees have been resistant so far to the mites and other issues that plague the honeybee, they, too, have suffered regional population declines due to habitat destruction and pesticide use. Humans are not the only ones that depend on bee pollination; so do many animal species that feed on bee-pollinated plants, and songbirds and fledglings that eat bees and their larvae.

The Melissa Garden: A Honeybee Sanctuary

In response to the honeybees' plight, some concerned beekeepers are pioneering a return to backyard beekeeping using more natural methods that support healthy beehives, methods that were common before the widespread use of pesticides. The Melissa Garden in Healdsburg, an enclave in Sonoma County's wine country, is just such a place. Barbara Schlumberger, the garden's visionary, teamed up with fellow beekeepers Priscilla Coe and Michael Thiele, a teacher of biodynamic beekeeping practices, to envision what a honeybee garden might look like. They brought in Kate Frey, an award-winning garden designer known for her pollinator gardens, to create a two-acre sanctuary where honeybees could live in as natural a state as possible. (Barbara's husband, Jacques, a beekeeper himself and owner of the Michel-Schlumberger Wine Estate, also hired Kate to design a pollinator garden at the winery to help balance the grape monoculture there.)

Lack of forage, says Barbara, is the most important underlying issue facing honeybees. She cites the practice of trucking 90 percent of the commercial honeybees to almond orchards in December, where they are fed high fructose corn syrup until the April bloom time, as not only stressful but "akin to having only apples to eat in our diet." Because honeybees eat what they are pollinating, a monoculture such as an almond orchard offers only one part of their

A Golden Hive, made in Germany, nestles among sunflowers and native madia (*Madia elegans*) in the Melissa Garden in Sonoma County, CA. PHOTOGRAPH BY KATE FREY.

nutritional needs. In the Melissa Garden, however, there is no lack of nutritious forage: honeybees (and native bees, butterflies, and other pollinators) feast on thickly planted drifts of every plant that honeybees not only like, but highly favor, their bloom times matched to the seasonal needs of the bees. A small meadow of native tansy-leaf phacelia (a most essential bee plant) creates a soft blur of blue and fast-moving wings from early spring right into summer. Out of the hundreds of mostly Mediterranean forage plants she grows, Barbara cites the following as other top attractors for honeybees: calamint, catmint, coffeeberry, cleome, sages, verbascum, lemon balm, native buckwheat, and sedums. One of her favorite plants, *Ceanothus* 'Gloire de Versailles', blooms all summer and is loved by all pollinators.

Several re-circulating fountains provide bees access to a source of water in the form of small, thick, floating cork pieces that bees can safely land on to draw up moisture. In this bee sanctuary the primary goal is not to harvest the honey (the bees need it to get through the winter); only the excess is taken. The bees make their own combs (conventional beekeepers use plastic combs) and they are allowed to swarm, which is the way bee colonies naturally multiply. Natural beekeeping practices such as these, combined with the Melissa Garden's natural beauty and vibrancy, draw hundreds of visitors to the tours and workshops offered here each year. (For a complete list of plants, see www. themelissagarden.com.)

Native Bees: Solitary and Nonaggressive

We have over 3,000 native bee species in this country—over 1,500 species in California alone—and they are very efficient pollinators. Estimates vary, but native bees may provide yearly pollinator services worth $3 billion. Studies show that native bee pollination has improved crop yields on agricultural lands near forests and wild grasslands, which has led some farmers to invest in hedgerows and habitat restoration to attract native pollinators. Unlike honeybees, most native bees are not social insects that live together in large colonies, but rather are solitary bees that nest in the ground or inside plant stems, wood or old beetle holes. They are not aggressive bees and their life cycles are short. Though males may pollinate flowers while they are waiting for females, the more reliable pollinators are the female bees, who make hundreds of trips carrying pollen from flowers to their nesting sites. Native bees don't produce honey and beeswax; they store pollen, which is high in protein and other nutrients, as a nutritious source of food for their larvae.

Over half of California's native bees are ground-nesters, so they need areas of undisturbed land to successfully complete their life cycles. Leaving some areas of the landscape bare and undisturbed, or lightly covered with leaf litter, allows native bees to burrow into the ground to make their nests. Decaying logs provide nesting sites as well. While some native bees are generalists, using almost any flower for a food source, others are specialists. Squash bees, for example pollinate only curcubits — squash, pumpkins, and gourds. To encourage native bees to set up residence in your wildlife garden, include native shrubs, perennials, and annuals that bloom from late winter through fall. Native bees have evolved with our native California plants; they are the ones that will attract the most diverse group of native bee species. In a study on native bees published in *Fremontia* magazine (July/October 2002), UC Berkeley entomologist Gordon Frankie reported that California native plants were four times more likely to attract native bees than exotic plants.

The early blooming native salvias — Brandegee sage, black sage, and purple sage, followed later by white sage and Cleveland sage — are magnets for native bees, as are early-flowering native trees and shrubs such as manzanita, California lilac, coffeeberry, willow, and others. Large drifts of pollen-rich native plants, such as sages, California poppy, tansy-

A native leafcutter bee, dusted with pollen, nectars on chicory, a non-native weed commonly found along roadsides.
PHOTOGRAPH BY BOB STEWART.

leaf phacelia, evening primrose (*Oenothera hookeri*), native buckwheat (*Eriogonum* spp.), asters, and other composites, will provide forage for native bees and honeybees. By carefully choosing plants that provide nectar and pollen through the seasons, and by gardening organically, we can help sustain honeybees and native bees, our most important pollinators. Restoration of habitat on agricultural lands, in developed communities, and in backyard gardens, and preservation of the wild habitat that still remains are all critical strategies to help ensure healthy populations of native bees. (See Appendix G, Top Nectar and Pollen Plant Families.)

Four Common Native Bee Species

Bumblebees. Bumblebee species (there are 26 native species in California) live in small colonies in the ground, and it is the queen who forms them each spring. Fertilized queens, who are the only survivors at the end of the year, hibernate until spring, when it's time to start up new colonies that may house as many as 100 bees. Once she has picked out a suitable nest, the queen forages on flowers for nectar and pollen, both of which she will bring back to the nest. The nectar is regurgitated for later use as nourishment. Pollen balls, a combination of nectar and pollen, will feed her brood when the eggs hatch; the nectar stored in a wax cell will provide a food source while she waits. Covered in fuzzy black-and-yellow hair, bumblebees range in size from 1/4 to 1 1/2 inches long. Native sages, bay trees, manzanitas, and rosemary are good early sources of nectar, though bumblebees are not specialists but will feed from a wide diversity of plants.

Carpenter bees. Sometimes called "robber bees," carpenter bees are known to slit flowers to obtain nectar, thereby "robbing" the flower of its pollination services. These bees are quite large (1/2 to 1 inch long) with a metallic sheen to their black bodies. They buzz loudly when they are flying, but they don't sting. Unlike other bees that nest in holes in old wood, carpenter bees can make their own holes or they may also choose bamboo stems for nests. Corn, pepper, pole beans, blackberries, and passionfruit are pollinated by carpenter bees.

Leaf-cutter bees. We have 60 species of leaf-cutter bees in California and they are particularly partial to pollen from the composites, members of the sunflower family. This small native bee's trademark is a little half-moon slice on the edge of a leaf, which it snips off to use as a partition between cells in its home, often an old beetle hole or hollow plant stem. Clarkia bees, one of the leaf-cutter species, are sometimes observed collecting clarkia petals for their cells.

Orchard mason bees. Manzanitas bloom at 55 degrees, around the time orchard mason bees emerge and are looking for food. Though it must be at least partly sunny for honeybees to be out and about, the orchard mason bee flies in any weather, from dawn to dusk. Though they only live six to eight weeks, mason bees are the most efficient pollinators for early blooming nut and fruit trees. Every female bee of this species is fertile. She uses old beetle holes, holes in dead wood, hollow reeds, or manmade boxes for nesting sites. She creates one cell for each egg, which is provisioned with pollen she brings back attached to her abdomen. The pollen is molded into a "loaf" as food for each cell, then the cell is sealed with mud. When all cells have been filled, the entrance to the nest is plugged. When the larvae have consumed the food supplies, they pupate in a silken cocoon until they transform into adults in late fall or winter. Males emerge first, but they wait for the females; the bees mate and the life cycle continues. These nonaggressive, solitary pollinators are blue in color and smaller than honeybees. Blue orchard bees, blueberry bees, and leaf-cutter bees are all part of the same bee family, Megachilidae.

Bees Are Not the Only Pollinators

Plants rely on the wind, birds, bees, and butterflies—and other pollinating insects—to transfer pollen from flower to flower. Some of our "other" pollinating insects are flies, wasps, and beetles. Though not all flies are pollinators, many are. With their black-and-yellow or black-and-

Hoverflies, which resemble bees, pollinate flowers; their larvae feed on aphids and other insects.
PHOTOGRAPH BY BOB STEWART.

white markings, hoverflies, also called "flower flies," are bee look-alikes. Hoverflies feed on nectar and pollinate many different flowers. Their larvae, however, eat large amounts of aphids. Almost all wasps, and there are over 3,000 different species in North America, visit flowers. Though yellow jackets do pollinate flowers, many pollinating wasps are tiny and nonaggressive. Like bees, they are attracted to fragrant flowers and bright colors. Pollinating beetles, which come in many different sizes and shapes, are attracted to spicy and fruity scented plants such as native spice bush (*Calycanthus occidentalis*), California poppies, California pipevine, and artichoke flowers.

Though both moths and butterflies are part of the order Lepidoptera, moths are far more numerous, with more than 10,000 species in North America and over 4,000 species in California. Many commonly found tiger moths are the adult forms of the fuzzy "woolly bear" caterpillars that seem to suddenly appear, intent on a destination, on foot trails and bike paths and other high-risk places. Some moths fly by day, such as the brightly colored Common Sheep moth, whose larvae feed on California lilac and wild roses. Most moths are nocturnal; they nectar on fragrant, light-colored flowers that open at dusk and close up in the day. Some moths are the only pollinators of one plant species. Each species of yucca, for example, has its own species of moth to pollinate it. The dreaded tomato hornworm turns into the largest of the Sphinx moths, important pollinators that hover like hummingbirds when they feed on deep-throated flowers such as the sages, and the *Agastache* and *Nicotiana* species. The White-lined Sphinx moth, the most common of the hawkmoths in California, displays a beautiful pink-and-white striped wing pattern. The easiest way to distinguish a moth from a butterfly is to get a glimpse of the antennae. Butterflies have a knob at the end of each antenna; moths have threadlike or feathered antennae. To bring in a diversity of pollinators, focus on a diversity of nectar plants—trees, shrubs, vines, and flowers—that are good sources of nectar and pollen through the seasons.

Insects: Foundation of Life in the Garden

Many of us have grown up believing that insects are the enemies of plants. Truth is insects and plants have a long relationship as partners. As renowned ecologist and author E.O. Wilson points out: "If plants, including many food and forage crops, as well as natural floras, must have insects to exist, then human beings must have insects to exist." They pollinate our plants, keep each other's numbers in check, and provide food for insect predators. Fundamentally, any garden is an ecosystem. Although it can never be as natural as Nature, the more it resembles Nature, the healthier it is. In the wildlife habitat garden, we look at the familiar "good bugs versus bad bugs" argument with a somewhat different perspective. Consider the view that all bugs have a job to do, including the bugs we label as "pests"—their job is to take out the weak, the unhealthy, and dying plants. If they are showing up in swarms, we need to look first at the cause (or causes) rather than the symptoms (leaf-chewing insects). We might start with a few questions: Is this plant unhealthy? Is it the right plant for the right place? Is it

A crab spider waits for its prey. PHOTOGRAPH BY BOB STEWART.

getting the right amount of sun, shade, or water? Plant-feeding insects are opportunists. They are highly attracted to plants that are weak or stressed or lush from being overwatered and overfertilized.

If a plant is unhealthy or poorly suited for the site, replacing it with a plant that is more site-appropriate is often the easiest and most sensible solution. All too often, however, the garden is seen as a battle-

ground. Eric Grissell, in his book *Insects and Gardens*, argues that not only is it a battle we can't win, but it is "unwise" and "virtually unnecessary." He would invite us to go into the garden, get friendly, and take the big view. After all, plants and insects have been evolving together, interacting in mutually beneficial ways, for thousands of years. Grissell wonders why we should "feel compelled to change this situation in an hour or afternoon."

Only a tiny percent of all insects (most experts agree that 90 percent or more of all insects are neutral or beneficial) are the ones we label "pests." When less desirable insects (from our point of view) are killed off, so are the beneficial insects that prey on them. A policy of prevention rather than intervention just makes sense. When you offer food and nectar plants for wildlife, you are inviting a balance of prey and predator into the garden. That balance of prey and predator combined with healthy soil and healthy plants means that insect intervention rarely becomes an issue. Keep in mind that there is, generally, a two-week lag time from when aphids show up on fresh new growth in early spring and when the beneficial insects arrive to prey on the aphids. As the aphid populations build up, a succession of "beneficials" show up to help manage them — ladybird beetles, lacewings, syrphid fly larvae, birds, and insectivores. On the other hand, a few holes could simply mean the work of a leaf-cutter bee, or if it is one of their larval host plants, a butterfly or moth caterpillar. Or it may simply signal that a thriving insect population, the foundation of the food web, is present. Not far away, especially if we've courted them, are their hungry predators.

Beneficial Insects: The Predators and the Parasitoids

Beneficial insects, insects that prey on other insects, use various methods to subdue their victims, many of which would make good fodder for a horror film. The *predator insects* simply kill their victims and then eat them. Sometimes the adults are the predators, sometimes the larvae, and sometimes, it's both. However, *parasitic insects* (parasitoids) lay eggs on or within their victim. The larvae of the parasitic insects then slowly feed on the living insect as it grows. Both predator and parasitic insects keep the leaf-chewing insects in balance, but they do not distinguish between "good" insects and "bad" insects. In the garden, almost everyone is someone else's lunch. Rejoice if the following beneficial insects are hard at work in your garden.

Green lacewing: Only the larvae of the green lacewing are the insect predators. Their menu consists mostly of aphids, scale insects, mealy bugs, and whiteflies. Lacewing larvae, nicknamed "aphid lions," resemble minuscule alligators. Lacewing eggs, hanging from long thin stalks on the underside of leaves, look like tiny white parachutes. (Ants, by the way, will eat lacewing eggs and will also defend aphids from predator insects.) The transparent, golden-eyed lacewing, 1/4- to 1/3-inch long, holds its wings tent-like over its body. Feeding on nectar and pollen, the adults live about two months.

Beneficial assassin bugs are fierce hunters that prey on many insects.
PHOTOGRAPH BY BOB STEWART.

Assassin bug: While all bugs are insects, not all insects are bugs. True bugs have piercing and sucking mouthparts, and the assassin bug is true to its name. This fierce hunter feeds on many insects, including tomato hornworms. As predatory insects, many assassin bugs have large, well-developed forelegs for grabbing prey. Others, however, have sticky, hairy legs instead.

Minute pirate bug: Adult minute pirate bugs and their larvae prey on leaf hoppers, thrips, spider mites, and many other arthropods. This beneficial insect is especially attracted to native buckwheat, such as the Santa Cruz buckwheat that blooms from late spring through summer.

Soldier beetles: Beetles, which are insects but not bugs, have mouthparts that are adapted for biting and chewing. Both adult soldier beetles and their larvae prey on the eggs and larvae of other insects. The long, slim adults, who visit flowers and eat pollen, catch their prey on plants. The larvae feed on insects in the soil.

Ground beetles: There are at least 800 species of ground beetles in

The larvae of ladybird beetles have voracious appetites for aphids. PHOTOGRAPH BY HARMINA MANSUR.

California and they are quite common in gardens. Both adults and larvae are active predators, hunting by night and hiding during the day under flowerpots or logs, or in rock piles and compost piles. Ground beetles eat whatever they can find, including slugs, cutworms, and moth larvae. Blue-black in color, often with a metallic sheen, many ground beetles are large insects with strong jaws.

Ladybird beetles: Ladybird beetles, or ladybugs, and their larvae are voracious aphid eaters. Some species eat scale, spider mites, and other small arthropods and their eggs, and they will also eat butterfly eggs and tiny caterpillars. Adult females lay up to 50 orange eggs per day. One ladybird beetle may consume as many as 400 aphids during its larval stage, which lasts almost a month. The adult, however, may live for almost a year. Unlike lacewings, purchased ladybugs generally fly away, but if you've got aphids in the garden, the ladybug's favorite meal, you have a good chance of attracting them and enticing them to stay and breed.

Rove beetles: Scavengers and beneficial decomposers, rove beetles help clean up decaying plant and animal material in the garden. You might find them in mulch and compost piles. Rove beetles, and there are close to 1,000 species in California, vary in size from tiny to large. They lay their eggs in soil, but only the adult beetles overwinter.

Parasitic wasps: Parasitic wasps do not sting, and there are many species of very tiny wasps only 1/50-inch long. They save their predatory instincts for caterpillars, aphids, sawfly borers, and other insects that serve

A ladybird beetle rests on a blanketflower bud (*Gaillardia* spp.). PHOTOGRAPH BY ROBERT WATKINS.

as hosts for their larvae. The adults, however, feed on pollen and nectar. Parasitic wasps are not social insects and are not aggressive. Even the larger predatory wasps (like paper wasps and yellow jackets) are valuable predators; they are aggressive to humans only when they feel threatened.

Hoverflies (AKA *flower flies, syrphid flies*): Bee look-alikes, adult hover-flies visit flowers to feed on pollen and lay their eggs. The green maggot-like larvae crawl along plants looking for aphids and other insects. Hoverflies are especially attracted to native plants such as ceanothus, coffeeberry, coyote bush, buckwheats, yarrow, and other composites.

Note: Please do not use zapper lights that electrocute insects. They are likely to kill more beneficial insects than pests.

Habitat for Beneficial Insects

Insects, the foundation of the food web, must be present if the beneficial insects—and birds, amphibians, and other insect predators—are to survive. Because aphids show up early in the year and because they reproduce so abundantly, aphid predators need early-blooming native trees and shrubs—ceanothus, hollyleaf cherry and other *Prunus* species, coffeeberry, elderberry, willow, manzanita—for shelter and food sources. Fall-blooming coyote bush is a magnet for insects and the predators that feed on them. Beneficial insects may supplement their diet with pollen, using many of the same plants that bees favor. Tiny pollinating flies and parasitic wasps are attracted to tiny flower clusters, such as thyme and mint flowers, or the commonly planted sweet alyssum. Native buckwheat species (*Eriogonum*) draw hoverflies, minute pirate bugs, lacewings, and many others. The umbels of carrot family members (Apiaceae) are especially appealing to beneficial insects and tiny polli-nators. Though the umbellifers, so-called for the umbrella shape of their flowers, have a short bloom period, they provide a large amount of nectar during that time. Try growing cow parsnip (*Heracleum lanatum*) and herbs such as parsley, dill, fennel, and lovage (*Levisticum officinale*), which resembles a very tall celery stalk. Bishop's flower (*Ammi majus*), which has fine, lacey white flowers and is very attractive to beneficial insects, is worth looking for in seed catalogs. Remember, of course, to let umbellifers flower and set seed! Composites—yarrow, aster, goldenrod, and many other members of the large sunflower family—are as equally appealing to beneficial insects looking for a supplemental food source as they are to bees and butterflies. (See Appendix G, Top Nectar and Pollen Plant Families.)

Cow parsnip and other umbellifers (members of the carrot family) attract tiny pollinators and beneficial insects.
PHOTOGRAPH BY JAMES HO.

Leaves, a renewable source of humus that many of us have in abundance, provide habitat for beneficial insects—rove beetles, soldier beetles, assassin bugs—that find a safe haven among leaf litter. Native bunchgrasses provide a refuge for ladybird beetles and many other insects. Old logs, a board on the ground, and rock piles provide permanent shelters for ground beetles, tiger beetles, ladybird beetles, and other beneficial insects. A pollinator garden is filled with daily drama. Consider investing in close-focus binoculars and a magnifying glass for delving more deeply into the fascinating life cycle of insects and their complex relationships with each other, with their prey and predators, and with the plants they depend on.

More Insect Predators

Birds. Many bird species feed mainly on insects. Other bird species supplement their seed or fruit diet with insects, and almost all bird species catch insects to feed their young. A single wren can consume more than 500 insect eggs, beetles, and grubs in one afternoon.

Garden spiders. One of the most effective garden predators, garden spiders eat moths, crickets, grasshoppers, and many other insects. Common garden spiders, such as wolf and crab spiders, are voracious predators of insects, and spider web work is particularly fascinating, especially when it sparkles with dew in early morning light!

Amphibians. Frogs, toads, and salamanders consume many thousands of insects and their eggs and larvae per year.

Reptiles. Lizards and snakes eat slugs, flies, cutworms, grasshoppers, and other invertebrates. Recent research shows that ticks that feast on the blood of the common Western Fence lizard are purged of any Lyme disease bacteria hiding in their gut. This fact may explain why there are fewer cases of Lyme disease in California than in states on the East Coast.

Bats. Bats feed on huge numbers of insects, especially mosquitoes and moths. Their droppings, or guano, are very high in nitrogen, which make them popular as a high quality plant fertilizer. Bat species are in decline and they suffer from the added disadvantage of having an undeserved reputation. Contrary to popular folklore, bats are shy creatures. According to the California Bat Conservation Fund only one bat in 1,000 that contracts rabies will become infected. Sick bats will fall to the ground and they should never be picked up or touched with bare hands, which is the only way bats can transmit a disease to humans. Bats are pollinators of fruit trees such as mangoes, dates, and avocados, and favor plants with sweet or fruity fragrances. They feed at dusk, using sonar to guide them to food sources.

Dragonflies. A dragonfly nymph (larva) can eat up to 300 mosquitoes during its aquatic stage, and adult dragonflies are highly effective predators of mosquitoes and other insects.

The Western Fence lizard, an effective insect predator, is a gardener's friend.
PHOTOGRAPH BY ROBERT WATKINS.

Charlotte's Habitat, Novato, Marin County

When Charlotte Torgovitsky and her husband saw their youngest child off for college in 2004, they moved to a two-acre hillside home in rural Marin County. Nestled in oak woodlands, this mostly sunny plot sits on a south-facing slope. An additional 50 acres of dedicated open space on the other side of the eastern boundary gradually slope downward to a series of wetlands 200 feet below. A veteran wildlife habitat gardener, Charlotte brought with her over 100 pots filled with rooted cuttings of her favorite wildlife habitat plants from her previous garden. After months of walking the property to figure out how wildlife habitat, a food garden, native plant communities, composting, and plant propagation would all fit together, Charlotte started with the front border. This wedge-shaped area, which was dominated by oleanders, society garlic, and a dozen massive echiums (*Echium candicans*), covers 60 feet in length and 40 feet at the widest end. The oleanders, which have little wildlife value, were the first to go. Although the echiums, an aggressive non-native shrub, were providing cover and nectar for insects and hummingbirds, they were gradually replaced to keep them from spreading to protected open space nearby.

Small trees and shrubs—redbud, *Arbutus* 'Marina', desert willow, hollyleaf cherry, and several buddleias (including *Buddleia salvifolia*)— were planted first, followed by groups of sages, lavenders, and one of Charlotte's favorite shrubs, *Lepechinia hastata*. A sweeping stand of Cleveland sage, deergrass, Pacific reed grass, and bur-marigold (*Bidens ferulifolia*) dominate the street-side edge of the border. Below this border, sloping downward toward the house, drifts of verbena, monkeyflower, blanketflower, and various grasses surround several large boulders. The gray-green color of five artemisias spread throughout the border creates a unifying effect. Though a color scheme was secondary to habitat value, orange monkeyflowers (*Mimulus aurantiacus*) grouped together with orange and pink *Agastache* 'Acapulco' make a stunning contrast to the artemisias and pale blue flowers of *Verbena rigida* 'Polaris' planted nearby. Currently, the percentage of California native plants in the front border, which is open to deer, is close to 70 percent. The balance of food and nectar plants is a mix of drought tolerant Mediterranean species that do not have a reputation for being invasive.

Rosemary, blooming in winter, drapes over a wooden retaining wall; a thicket of fragrant coyote mint (*Monardella villosa*) spills over another. One of Charlotte's favorite summer-blooming wildflowers, *Madia elegans*, has seeded itself in the gravel along the edges of the driveway and elsewhere in the garden. As no landscaping fabric was used under the gravel, seedlings grow in this "seed bed" along the edges of the paths. Some volunteers stay where they are; others are dug up for potting or

Drifts of monkeyflowers, sages, verbenas, and other nectar plants attract many pollinators. PHOTOGRAPH BY MIEKO WATKINS.

transplanting to different locations. Using the native plant communities on nearby Mt. Burdell as inspiration, Charlotte interplanted wildflowers with the native purple needlegrass growing along the woodland edges of the property. She grows creambush (*Holodiscus discolor*), hazelnut (*Corylus cornuta*), and bush monkeyflower (*Mimulus aurantiacus*) under the oaks on the property and has added drifts of native coral bells, a dry shade plant, for color. A tiny frog pond, a birdbath, and a cascading series of small ponds in the back garden provide a constant source of fresh water for birds and other wildlife. The frog pond, planted with creek monkeyflower (*Mimulus guttatus*) and mare's tail (*Hippuris vulgaris*), includes a bog area and tiny gravel beach that allows access to insects and birds. Water flows through the bog and spills out over the beach once a day, which ensures that no mosquito larvae will hatch. Overlapping layers of trees, shrubs, perennials, and annuals create multiple nesting sites, cover, and places for wildlife to forage. This garden habitat, a dazzling blend of rich textures, fragrance, foliage, and color, blends harmoniously with the rich background tapestry of oaks and grasslands.

Wildlife focus: A myriad of nectar and butterfly host plants brings in many butterflies (19 species are seen regularly). Larvae of the Anise Swallowtail, Monarch, Painted Lady, American Lady, Mylitta Crescent,

Cabbage White, and Common Buckeye butterflies have been found in the garden. Orange Sulfurs and California Ringlets, which find their caterpillar food plants in the grasslands nearby, are frequently seen nectaring. Because the Mylitta Crescent butterfly and many beneficial insects use the Italian thistles that grow at the edges of the property, Charlotte has allowed a few stands of this weed to remain. The abundance of butterfly larval food and nectar plants in this garden also feeds honeybees, native bees, and other beneficial insects through the seasons. In Charlotte's garden, bees are particularly fond of drifts of spring-blooming rosemary, fall-blooming madia and coyote mint, and *Ceanothus* 'Gloire de Versailles', a beautiful and highly fragrant summer-blooming hybrid.

Barn Owls (two nest boxes were set up in open space nearby) have been breeding on the land successfully for the past six years, fascinating the family with their calls and courting behaviors in January and, later, with flying lessons for the fledglings. Tree Swallows, Titmice, Western Bluebirds, and Ash-throated Flycatchers have also bred in the nest boxes hung for them around the garden and in the woodland. More than 36 species of birds have been observed feeding on the seeds of composites in the fall and on the many insects that the plants attract. All insects are welcome; problem pests are quickly taken care of by their natural predators. The dry-stack method used for the retaining walls and planter beds offers many hiding places for lizards and skinks. The irregular stone surfaces also make shallow pools of water available to small creatures. Native Pacific Chorus frogs are abundant in the garden.

Special features: Charlotte and her husband installed an "invisible" deer fence to surround the food garden, approximately half an acre. The materials include nine-foot-tall metal poles, metal "sleeves," and heavy black plastic netting. Taking care not to obstruct any major deer paths, Charlotte tied white strips of cloth on the fencing every 30 feet to make the fence visible to the deer, and they have never come through it. A vegetable garden that provides food for the table year-round, fruit trees (including fig, guava, and persimmon), and berry bushes are part of the food forest Charlotte has created in the back garden. Interplanted with the veggies are culinary and medicinal herbs, and annuals such as sunflowers, nasturtiums, and cosmos. Along the inside of

OPPOSITE PAGE: A drift of summer-blooming coyote mint (*Monardella villosa*) provides nectar for pollinators and seeds for birds. BELOW: *Salvia microphylla* 'Hot Lips' blooms from spring through late fall, attracting hummingbirds, bees, and other pollinators. PHOTOGRAPHS BY MIEKO WATKINS.

the fence, Charlotte has planted a native plant hedgerow of ceanothus, California rose, coffeeberry, blue elderberry, toyon, currants, grasses, and wildflowers.

Plant installation: Charlotte and her son, Anders, a garden designer, brought in enriched loam to build up berms and rock dust to supply minerals to the native clay soil. Locally mined basalt was used for terracing the front border above the house; steps and pathways were built with a combination of flagstone and gravel. Charlotte did all of the planting, using mostly plants she has propagated from seed or cuttings. In-line drip irrigation systems are used throughout the garden areas, except for areas around oaks. A product called Dri-Water® was used for new shrubs near or under oaks for the first two summers. Mini-sprinklers are used temporarily to germinate wildflower seeds in the fall and to provide extra moisture for plants as they establish. As native plants get established, watering is reduced or cut off.

Garden practices: Charlotte applies mulch or compost (alternately each year) to the soil and adds a screened green mulch to flower beds on a biennial basis or, occasionally, as a top dressing. Leaf litter is left under the native oaks, but mulch is never applied. Non-native annual grasses in border areas, weeded before they go to seed, are composted in place along with a little straw. Because of this practice, purple needlegrass and many species of wildflowers dominate the oak understory from spring through fall. Rock dust is applied in all new planting areas and each year in the vegetable beds where only compost, worm tea, and horse manure are used as fertilizers. No pesticides, herbicides, or other chemicals are used anywhere in the garden. Charlotte strives to create a garden that encourages diverse populations of insects; not just the pollinators and decomposers and other beneficial insects but aphids, too, are welcome because they and other plant-eaters are the foundation of all other life that exists in this garden habitat.

Favorite plants: For their form, flower, and fragrance, for their variable bloom times, and because they are easy to propagate, salvias top the list of Charlotte's favorite habitat plants. She can count on roseleaf sage (*Salvia involucrata*) for fall bloom, *S. iodantha* for flowers in the coolest months of winter, and Brandegee sage (*S. brandegeei*) for providing early spring nectar. One of her favorites, *S. melissodora*, blooms almost all year with pretty, light-blue flowers.

Rewards: One of the many bird species that feasts on the insect population in this garden is the Ash-throated Flycatcher, one of Charlotte's favorite birds and the only member of the Myiarchus in her area. "I first saw this species," says Charlotte, "at Lake Pillsbury in Mendocino National Forest, where my husband and I camp in the summer. I was thrilled when I heard their call, a series of short, somewhat musical gurgles, in our own woods a couple of years ago. The flycatchers were inspecting a large live oak for suitable nesting cavities. There were none, so in the fall I hung a nesting box in that same oak. The following year in early May they were back! Within the month they found 'their box'; the female built her nest, laid eggs, and by mid-June the pair was busy catching insects for their hungry nestlings." Charlotte has taken her passion for wildlife habitat gardening into the community as an educator, teaching classes on wildlife gardening, composting, and propagating native plants—and by sharing her garden on Marin County's Eco-friendly Garden Tour. (See Charlotte's propagating tips in Appendix A, Natural Gardening Guidelines.)

OPPOSITE: Rosebud sage (*Salvia involucrata*), which needs little water, is a favorite of hummingbirds in the fall. PHOTOGRAPH BY MIEKO WATKINS.

The Ash-throated Flycatcher and many other bird species feed mainly on insects. PHOTOGRAPH BY ROBERT WATKINS.

Charlotte's Garden: Front Border Plant List

All of the plants in this list are deer-proof or deer-resistant. Some plants are tip-pruned by deer at various times, which stimulates growth and does not harm the plant. General bloom periods and wildlife value are noted.

* California native plants

Trees and Shrubs

Arbutus 'Marina'. Fall and winter bloom; bees, hummingbirds, fruit for birds

*Bush mallow (*Malacothamnus fremontii*). Summer; butterflies, bees, birds, host plant for Painted Lady and West Coast Lady butterflies

Butterfly bush (*Buddleia davidii, B. salvifolia*). Summer; pollinators, hummingbirds

*California lilac (*Ceanothus* 'Dark Star'—deer resistant species). Early spring; pollinators/insects, host plant for Spring Azure, California Tortoiseshell, California Hairstreak, Hedgerow Hairstreak, Brown Elfin butterflies

*Desert willow (*Chilopsis linearis*). Summer; hummingbirds

*Hollyleaf cherry (*Prunus ilicifolia*). Spring; pollinators/insects, fruit for birds, host plant for Pale Swallowtail butterfly

*Island mallow (*Lavatera/Malva assurgentiflora*). Summer; pollinators, host plant for West Coast and Painted Ladies

*Manzanitas (*Arctostaphylos densiflora* 'Howard McMinn' and 'Sentinel'). Late winter; bees, hummingbirds, beneficial insects

*Mountain mahogany (*Cercocarpus betuloides*). Summer; pollen source

*Oak spp. Blue oak (*Quercus douglasii*), Oregon oak (*Q. garryana*), coast live oak (*Q. agrifolia*). Oaks are host plants for California

Sister, Mournful Duskywing, Propertius Duskywing butterflies, and many moth species; birds, insects, acorns in fall

*Redbuds (*Cercis canadensis, C. occidentalis*). Early spring; hummingbirds

Sages (*Salvia clevelandii*, *S. brandegeei*, *S. leucophylla* 'Pt. Sal Spreader' and 'Figueroa', *S. apiana*, *S. mellifera*, *S. melissodora*, *S. iodantha*, *S. canariensis*, *S.* 'Hot Lips', *S. greggii*, *S. buchanii*). All seasons; hummingbirds, bees, insects

*Silk tassel bush (*Garrya elliptica*). Late winter; insects, birds, pollinators

Perennials and Annuals

Blanketflower (*Gaillardia* spp.). Spring through fall; planted in drifts, butterflies, bees, beneficial insects

Bur marigold (*Bidens ferulifolia*). Summer; spreading ground cover, butterflies, bees, beneficial insects

*Bush monkeyflower (*Mimulus aurantiacus* and hybrids). Spring/fall; planted in drifts, hummingbirds/pollinators, host plant for Variable Checkerspot, Common Buckeye butterflies

*California sagebrush (*Artemisia californica* 'Montara'). Planted as accents and cover

*Cobweb thistle (*Cirsium occidentale*). Spring; scattered in small drifts, host plant for Painted Lady and Mylitta Crescent butterflies, seeds and nesting materials for birds

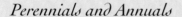

*Coyote mint (*Monardella villosa*). Summer through fall; planted in drifts, butterflies/pollinators

*Foothill penstemon (*Penstemon heterophyllus*). Spring through summer; hummingbirds, pollinators, host plant for Common Buckeye butterfly

Goldenrods (*Solidago californica, S. rugosa*). Fall; planted in drifts, butterflies, bees, beneficials; *S. rugosa* forms groundcover

Lavender (*Lavandula* 'Provence'). Summer; repeated accents, butterflies/pollinators, beneficial insects

*Pitcher sages (*Lepechinia hastata, L. calycina*). Fall; planted in drifts, hummingbirds; *L. calycina* blooms early summer

Rosemary (*Rosmarinus* 'Tuscan Blue'; *R.* 'Irene' covers the retaining wall). Late winter; bees, beneficial insects

*St. Catherine's lace and rosy buckwheat (*Eriogonum giganteum, E. grande rubescens*). Fall; bees, butterflies, and other pollinators; top butterfly nectar plants

*Showy milkweed and narrowleaf milkweed (*Asclepias speciosa, A. fascicularis*). 30 plants of *A. fascicularis* scattered in groups throughout the site; *A. curassavica* planted in pots only. Summer; host plant for Monarch butterfly, bees, butterflies, other insects

*Tarweeds (*Madia elegans, Hemizonia* spp.). Summer/fall; butterflies, bees, beneficial insects; tarweeds have planted themselves throughout the garden

Verbenas (*Verbena bonariensis, V. rigida*). Summer; planted in drifts, butterflies and other pollinators

Grasses

Host plants for grass skippers and California Ringlet butterflies; cover, seed, and nesting materials for birds.

*Deergrass (*Muhlenbergia rigens*), *Calamagrostis nutkaensis* 'The King', *Calamagrostis foliosa, Stipa gigantea*, *purple needlegrass (*Nassella pulchra* — butterfly host plant for California Ringlet), blue oat grass (*Helictotrichon sempervirens*), *California meadow sedge (*Carex pansa*); *California fescue (*Festuca californica*), which likes some shade and no summer water, is planted under oaks in the front garden.

Stands of native evening primrose (*Oenothera hookeri*), in the author's garden, attract native bees and other pollinators; finches eat the seeds for many months.
PHOTOGRAPH BY NANCY BAUER.

CHAPTER 4

The Wildlife Pond

I cannot imagine living without a wildlife pond.

— Kathy Biggs, wildlife habitat gardener

Water cools and invigorates. It warms, renews, and heals. Whether trickling over stones, catching the sunlight, or murmuring its soothing melody, water in its many incarnations entices us to come closer, to dip in a hand or toe, to wade around perhaps, or just sit on a boulder and watch it float by. Water is universally appealing in the wild and in the garden—to people *and* to wildlife—and it is essential for life. In addition to attracting many bird species, a pond may bring in other wildlife that you might not otherwise see in your garden. With wetland habitat disappearing—even drainage ditches— ponds are oases for local and migrating birds, tree frogs, foxes, and other local creatures. If there's a local population anywhere nearby, jewel- toned dragonflies and their relatives, the damselflies, may be the first visitors to your pond.

Wildlife Pond Basics

Wildlife ponds have little in common with koi ponds. Though koi are beautiful creatures, they are not compatible with wildlife. They eat almost anything, including the pond plants that provide cover and shade for dragonfly larvae, tadpoles, and other aquatic creatures. Herons and raccoons, which consider koi gourmet fare, are not welcome. Ornamental ponds are also costly to set up and care for; wildlife ponds, on the other hand, are relatively easy to create and maintain. Expenses for a wild- life pond are minimal. As one backyard "ponder" put it: "I acquired my

OPPOSITE: In the fall at the Biggses' pond (see Garden Profile, p. 116), the Japanese maple turns red and the large leaves of Indian rhubarb (*Darmera peltata*) begin to turn golden. PHOTOGRAPH BY DAVE BIGGS.

107

Many food and nectar plants, including cardinal flower, milkweed, and buckwheat, surround this wildlife pond. PHOTOGRAPH BY STEVE HARPER.

pond as a birthday present from the two guys in my life, my husband and son. All it required was an afternoon, a shovel, and a pond liner." Even a pump is not necessary, except to provide moving water to create a waterfall. What *is* necessary are plants—emergent and floating plants that cover approximately 60 percent of the surface, and some oxygenating underwater plants.

Although ponds of any size will attract wildlife, the larger the pond, the more stable the water temperature and pond ecosystem. Preformed ponds are easy solutions for small areas or where a larger pond is not feasible. As wildlife ponds, however, they have some serious drawbacks. Preformed ponds have smooth, steep sides, which limit accessibility for wildlife to safely bathe and drink. Should an animal fall in, the steep sides often prevent escape. Size options are limited and once camouflaged with plants and rocks, they tend to look much smaller than their original size. If you choose a preformed pond, a branch partially submerged in the pond offers an escape route. Rigid pond liners also have a tendency to leak or crack; well-packed sand around the edges helps ameliorate this problem. Concrete ponds, another option, must be very carefully installed to prevent leaks. They are likely to crack in an earthquake and are difficult to repair. Also, concrete ponds must be sealed to prevent chemicals from leaching into the water.

By far the material of choice for ponds is the EDPM flexible rubber liner (45 ml is often recommended). It not only has a long life span but can also be arranged to form ponds or streams of many different sizes and shapes. Be sure to check for stones and roots before laying down the liner. *Tip:* Layers of newspapers or an old carpet under the liner helps protect the liner from rocks poking through. If possible, make your pond at least 18 inches to two feet in the center, though a three-foot depth in the middle of the pond increases the area of safety for pond inhabitants. Deeper ponds also discourage raccoons from rearranging the pond plants. Books and websites are available on how to build a pond; however, the following suggestions will help ensure that you—and the local wildlife—get the most out of

Dragonflies are often the first visitors to a wildlife pond. Pictured here are the Twelve-spotted Skimmer (top) and the Flame Skimmer (bottom). PHOTOGRAPHS BY DAVE BIGGS.

your pond experience. *Note: Be sure to check county or city ordinances before building a pond. The same safety precautions for swimming pools should be observed for ponds of any size: both swimming pools and ponds are unsafe for unsupervised children.*

Build your pond where you can see it. If the pond is out of sight, it will most likely be neglected, and most certainly not enjoyed. One

couple positioned a couch near a window overlooking their wildlife pond and that spot, they report, is where everyone who visits wants to sit! Be sure a hose is readily available for topping off pond water.

Choose a sunny site. Ponds need at least a half-day of sunlight. As long as most of the pond is in sunlight, trees or shrubs may shade other parts of the pond. As warmer water fosters the growth of algae, it's helpful to have the west side of the pond shaded from afternoon heat. Avoid, if possible, placing your pond under a tree where it may receive too much shade—and a profusion of leaves in the fall. Digging too close to trees may also harm their roots.

Create a more natural look with uneven pond edges. Flat rocks, boulders, pieces of driftwood, logs, or other woody debris soften the edges and more closely mimic a wild pond. A branch or old log that is partially submerged in the water creates a nice visual effect and also allows an easy escape route from the water. Grasses, sedges, and shrubs near the pond offer perching spots for dragonflies and foraging sites for insects and other wildlife. Varied edges increase entry points for amphibians, birds, and small mammals.

Provide a beach. A sloping beach that leads to shallow water at the edge of the pond allows birds and other wildlife easy and safe access for drinking and bathing. It also makes it easier for you to wade in to work in the pond. Even more importantly, the shallow beach area and sloping sides around the pond offer an escape route for small animals that might fall in. Steep sides may prevent raccoons from re-arranging the plants, but they may also trap an animal that falls in.

Cover two-thirds of the pond with vegetation. Pond plants provide breeding sites for dragonflies and hiding and foraging sites for dragonfly larvae, called *nymphs*, and other aquatic creatures. The plants act as a water filter and provide shade, which keeps pond temperatures lower, and they absorb some of the nutrients in the water that algae thrive on.

Floating and emergent plants should cover approximately two-thirds of the water surface—underwater plants the remaining one-third—to maintain a balanced ecosystem. Underwater plants, such as water purslane and waterweed, are oxygenators; they should be completely submerged and planted first. Underwater plants can be started on a plastic seedling tray (with drainage holes) in shallow water deep enough to cover the plants. Place rocks on top to weigh down the plants so they don't float away. Once plants are established, they can be moved into deeper water.

Floating plants include plants that are rooted in soil with their leaves floating on the surface, such as water lilies. Free-floating water hyacinths

OPPOSITE: Emergent plants, such as Western blue flag iris (*Iris missouriensis*), provide hiding places for pond creatures and breeding sites for dragonflies. THIS PAGE: A damselfly nymph emerges from the Biggses' wildlife pond (see Garden Profile, p. 116). PHOTOGRAPHS BY DAVE BIGGS.

are widely available but they are not a good choice for wildlife ponds. They are extremely aggressive plants that can quickly take over a pond, requiring frequent weeding and removal in order to keep the pond in balance. Too often, invasive non-native aquatic plants such as water hyacinth find their way into our waterways. In Nature every wild pond is in the process of becoming a meadow with accumulating sediment and plant debris, but we can avoid that proclivity when creating a wildlife pond. Tiny-leaved, free-floating plants such as duckweed and water fern are also aggressive, and they can quickly take over a pond's surface. Both plants can be easily removed with a net, and excess amounts of these nutrient-rich plants make excellent compost or mulch for garden plants. However, vigilance and regular maintenance are essential, especially in small ponds. When removing any plants from the pond, use a shallow tray, wire mesh basket or screen for plant debris and always check for frog eggs, dragonfly nymphs, and other aquatic insects. Place the tray or basket near or over the pond surface to allow creatures to escape back into the water. If the pond must be completely drained (typically at three- to six-year intervals), drain water slowly so pond creatures can hide in the deeper water. Save plants and as many pond creatures as possible in buckets or holding tanks. Avoid cleaning ponds in spring when frog eggs are in the pond and dragonfly nymphs are emerging.

Emergent plants, such as mare's tail, water plantain, and blue flag iris, grow above the level of the pond. They are rooted in pots that should be submerged an inch or so below the level of the pond. Use heavy clay soil (finer soil will float away) and cover the top of the pots with small stones. A handful of pebbles at the bottom of the container will make it more stable in water. Large, flat rocks can be used for the deep areas of the pond as pedestals for pots. *Note:* Look for soft-sided planting bags or "slotted" pots that are specifically designed for water gardens at hardware stores and pond shops. Regular plastic one-gallon garden pots can be cut off at the top to make them more stable in the pond.

Consider adding a waterfall. The sound of moving water is appealing to both people and wildlife, but pumps for wildlife ponds are

Pacific Chorus Frogs

Our native Pacific Chorus frogs, also called *tree frogs*, almost always find backyard wildlife ponds. These small frogs, up to only several inches in length, are common along the West Coast from British Columbia to Baja California. Though the females breed in water and lay their eggs on pond vegetation, tree frogs spend most of their time on land in various, often woodland, habitats. During the day they may hide out under rocks or logs, in the crevices of stone walls, in flowerpots, or other dark moist places. Though all Pacific Chorus frogs share a distinctive black stripe that runs from nose through eye to shoulder, body color can vary from shades of tan and gray to reddish bronze and lime green. That color may also change at times to blend in with the frog's surroundings.

In late winter or early spring, the males find water and call to the females with a chorus of frog music. Eggs are attached to pond vegetation and tadpoles emerge within several weeks and begin feeding on pond algae. When tadpoles transform into "froglets" two months later, they move away from the ponds to feed on mosquitoes and other tiny insects. Adult frogs stay on the land until it's time to return to water in late winter or spring to breed again. Ephemeral wetlands are natural habitat for Pacific Chorus frogs; preserving them is vital for the health of native frog populations. Like all amphibians, tree frogs need a clean environment and are especially sensitive to pesticides.

A male Pacific Chorus frog sings to attract females to this wildlife pond. PHOTOGRAPH BY PAT HUNT.

optional. Although a pump is not necessary to keep the water clear in a natural pond, a re-circulating pump does increase oxygenation in the pond, and water movement discourages mosquitoes from breeding and helps control algal bloom build-up.

Weigh the pros and cons of fish. Fish are often added to ponds to control mosquitoes, but fish also eat the eggs and larvae of dragonflies and damselflies, frog eggs and tadpoles. Introduced into California in the 1920s for their insatiable appetites for mosquito larvae, mosquito fish (*Gambusia affinis*) can consume hundreds of larvae per day. They also have insatiable appetites for frog eggs, polliwogs, dragonfly eggs, and nymphs. So do goldfish. Algae-eating mollies, however, seem to be less devastating to breeding frog and dragonfly populations. Mosquito dunks (*Bacillus thuringiensis israelensis*) are an effective alternative to fish. BTi mosquito disks, which are widely available at hardware stores and pond shops, kill *only* the larval stage of members of the Diptera family (mosquitoes, black flies, and crane flies) and will not harm tadpoles, dragonfly nymphs, or other wildlife. Before adding fish to a pond filled with chlorinated water, be sure to wait several days to allow the chlorine to evaporate. If you are filling your pond with chlorinated water, consider using a de-chlorinator. *Note:* Check with your municipal water district to find out if chloramines (a compound of chlorine and ammonia) are used to disinfect the water supply. Chloramines dissipate much more slowly than chlorine and should be removed, as they are harmful to fish, frogs, and other aquatic life. Commercial products are available at pond shops and garden centers for removing chlorine and chloramines.

Add a bog to extend the habitat value of the pond. Bog areas around the pond extend wildlife habitat even farther, and they help tie the pond to the rest of the landscape. Planting around the edges of the pond hides the liner and makes the pond look established more quickly. Create bogs by covering a one-foot to 18-inch deep hole with a pond liner. Punch out drainage holes on the bottom of the liner before filling with a mixture of soil, compost, peat, and water. Extend the liner at the edges to give bog plants room to spread. Bogs planted with nectar flowers, ferns, and grasses offer cover, shade and foraging areas. Swamp

milkweed (*Asclepias incarnata*), water hyssop (*Bacopa monnieri*), cardinal monkeyflower (*Mimulus cardinalis*), creek monkeyflower (*M. guttatus*), marsh marigold (*Caltha palustris*), and bog sage (*Salvia uliginosa*) are examples of moisture-loving plants that attract birds, butterflies, and other insects.

Let the pond develop naturally. At the beginning, an algal bloom is part of the pond's evolution toward stability. Small amounts of leaves and algae are natural to ponds and keep them healthy and in balance. Avoid using chemicals to kill algae; they will also kill pond life. A pond net, however, is handy for cleaning out the excess. Backyard ponders differ in their approach to pond maintenance: some thin plants and clean out leaves twice a year; others clean less often. Generally, when the pond finds its balance, prey and predator, too, find a balance.

Creek monkeyflower (*Mimulus guttatus*) provides cover and nectar in the bog section of the Biggses' pond (see Garden Profile, p.116).
PHOTOGRAPH BY DAVE BIGGS.

The Biggses' Pond, Sebastopol, Sonoma County

Not long after their boys moved out, Kathy and Dave Biggs decided to turn their above-ground swimming pool into a wildlife pond. Located just past the backyard deck, only yards from the kitchen window, the pond takes center stage for an impressive cast of players. Though the size of their pond was predetermined—it measures 20 x 24 feet—it turned out to be very close in size to what the British Dragonfly Society has determined works best for dragonflies (15 x 20 feet). Perhaps, then, it is no coincidence that dragonflies were the very first visitors to the Biggses' wildlife pond in the spring of 1996. They did no less than change the lives of Kathy and her husband, Dave. As she became more and more fascinated with these acrobatic insects, Kathy attempted to identify them. As there were no field guides available at the time, she began to do her own research. Four years later she published the first edition of *Common Dragonflies of California.* It was just the beginning. In the years that followed, Kathy found herself booked from spring through fall giving dragonfly programs and leading field tours. Somewhere in between she tackled the dragonfly species of the Southwest and published a second guide. When she first started, Kathy recalls, there were just a few

dragonfly enthusiasts exchanging information via email. Times have changed. Over the past 10 years, Kathy's dragonfly website has averaged over 1,000 hits per day, and numerous regional and national dragonfly field guides are now available.

Pond installation: The Biggses spent several months researching pond literature and observing numerous ponds in the wild before embarking on their project. Though there was scant information on wildlife ponds at that time, Kathy learned about the importance of a

Kathy and Dave Biggs enjoy watching the action on the pond from the patio and the deck. PHOTOGRAPH BY PATRICK KINCAID.

shallow beach area and sloping pond sides. When the owners took down the metal sides of the above-ground pool, they left the liner in the ground to become the deep end of the pond. From the beach area, the pond moves gradually from outside shallow areas only several inches deep to the deepest area, at about three feet. A planting shelf was built around the perimeter of the pond at the 18-inch mark to hold aquatic plant containers. The shallow beach area, covered with river stones, offers wildlife easy entry to the pond for bathing and drinking. A gnarled manzanita branch bisects the edge of the pond, offering an escape route while also adding a natural touch. Because pond liners become slippery with algae and plant debris, the owners used sand bags (burlap bags filled with soil) as steps into the deepest part of the pond from the beach area. The steps, placed between the pond liner and pond bottom, make entry into the pond much easier when pond maintenance is required.

Instead of decorating the pond edges with pavers, the owners chose

to make their pond look more natural by adding rocks and boulders. A log anchors the front of the pond and makes a perfect bench for lounging, feet dangling in the water, on a warm summer day. Rocks that were placed around the edges of the pond are held in place with expanding spray foam insulation, a nontoxic type that becomes inert once it dries. (Cement, which leaches chemicals into the pond, should be avoided.) At the beginning, Kathy stocked the pond with fish. Because the number of dragonflies and Pacific Chorus frogs successfully breeding in the pond plummeted after the introduction of fish, Kathy painstakingly removed them all and now relies on mosquito dunks (in addition to frogs and dragonflies) for mosquito control.

Pond and bog plants: Planting shelves that were built around the perimeter of the pond are used for one-gallon pots (squat soft-sided pots are more stable than conventional containers) filled with clumps of emergent and floating plants. Dragonflies need plants above the water line to perch on, and dragonfly nymphs need at least one emergent vertical plant to crawl up on when they leave the water. Because it spreads so quickly, Kathy grows native horsetail (*Equisetum* spp.) in a pot on the deck above the pond. Dragonflies find it handy as a perch while waiting for insects. Aquatic plants include blue flag iris, pond pickerelweed, arrowhead, native creeping water primrose, mare's tail, water plantain (the Spread-winged Damselfly's favorite plant), water clover, and *Elodea canadensis*, an underwater plant. Bogs on opposites sides of the pond catch the overflow when the pond is full. The sunny bog is planted with creek monkeyflower and marsh marigold; the shadier bog is a mix of Indian rhubarb and ferns. Kathy has chosen California natives and other aquatic plants native to North America for their easy care and their value to wildlife.

Special feature: The owners constructed a waterfall with four boulders: two boulders form the base of the waterfall and a cup-shaped boulder, the top. A fourth boulder placed to the left of the waterfall completes the design. Dark-colored flexible piping, placed in a deep area on the opposite side of the pond, connects the circulating pump to the waterfall. The splitter at the end of the tubing atop the boulders was

LEFT: Kathy Biggs cools off in the pond while thinning some of the pond plants. PHOTOGRAPH BY DAVE BIGGS.

concealed beneath several flat rocks. The soothing sound of the waterfall brings in many species of birds to drink and bathe, all with different preferences. Towhees, for example, always choose the shallow beach area, but hummingbirds and warblers bathe in the shallow basin at the top of the waterfall.

Pond maintenance: Kathy enters the pond as infrequently as possible and never in spring when the delicate eggs of the Pacific Chorus frog are attached to plants. She thins pond plants when needed in summer or fall and puts the trimmings in a bucket next to the pond in the sun. At the end of the day, dragonfly nymphs and other insects will have moved to the sunny side of the bucket where they can be removed and returned to the pond. Excess leaves are scooped out with a net and carefully checked for pond life before being composted.

Wildlife focus: Over 50 bird species have been seen at the Biggses' pond, from the "regulars"—California Towhees, Black Phoebes, Titmice—to seasonal migrants, such as Cedar Waxwings, Ash-throated Flycatchers, Townsend's Warblers, and Ruby-crowned Kinglets.

Mallards, herons, and hawks occasionally visit. Because many mature trees, shrubs, berry bushes, and fruit trees grow behind the pond and throughout the back yard, local and migrant birds gather at all levels of these vertical layers from season to season, looking for insects and feeding on berries and seeds. Various local butterflies have been observed "puddling" on the moist sand in the shallow beach area. Fox families are regular visitors and, of course, raccoons (Kathy refers to them as "the great re-arrangers") show up after dark. While some backyard ponders discourage raccoons or, at the very least, grumble about them, Kathy takes a different view. She bestows ownership of the pond to her wildlife visitors, and reserves the role of pond steward for herself. Pacific Chorus frogs discovered the pond immediately and set up housekeeping. Though

the native frogs live on land, they return to the pond to breed and lay their eggs on pond vegetation.

With all of its varied wildlife this pond is, above all else, a certifiable and wildly successful dragonfly pond! Twenty-six species of dragonflies and damselflies have been counted. Pondhawks, dashers, skimmers, darners, and damselflies consistently breed in the pond. Tiny Pacific Forktails, the first to show each year, signal that summer is on its way. By mid-summer, the bright red Cardinal Meadowhawks, known at the Biggses' pond as the "Red Barons," are dueling over pond positions. Once, after a wind storm had moved out, the biggest prize of all showed up—a San Francisco Forktail, the rarest damselfly in North America!

The rewards: "I had always thought butterfly metamorphosis was the miracle," says Kathy, "but the dragonfly that changes in just one hour from underwater nymph to a flying, air-breathing creature is no less a miracle. Having a wildlife pond has enriched my life way beyond expectations. Our retirement home is not yet finished, but the wildlife pond is already in!"

FACING PAGE: California Towhees prefer the shallow water near the "beach" for bathing. THIS PAGE: The wildlife pond the Biggses built at their retirement home near Mt. Shasta attracts many migrant bird species, deer, the occasional coyote and, so far, one black bear! PHOTOGRAPHS BY DAVE BIGGS.

Dragonflies

Dragonflies and damselflies, members of the insect order Odonata, have been with us since prehistoric times, even before the dinosaurs. Though we know them as acrobatic flyers, these fascinating and aggressive insect predators actually live underwater much longer than they breathe air. Hiding out in pond debris and underwater vegetation, dragonfly nymphs prey on mosquito larvae, aquatic insects, tadpoles, even tiny fish. They may spend only a winter underwater or as long as two or more years. After the dragonfly nymph emerges on a plant stem to shed its skin above water, it may live as an adult for only a few weeks longer.

Pictured here are Cardinal Meadowhawk dragonflies mating in the "wheel" position. PHOTOGRAPH BY RAY BRUUN.

Male dragonflies, vigorously defending their territories, station themselves around streams, ponds, and lakes. When mating, the male grabs the female behind her eyeballs, using appendages at the end of his abdomen. If she is willing, they contort into the heart-shaped mating wheel position. The male dragonfly, however, has another unusual mating tool that he may employ before insemination. This tool, located under his second abdominal segment, is used to remove any sperm inside the female that may have been deposited from another male. Some female dragonflies lay their eggs directly into the water or on aquatic plants. Others place their eggs into slits they cut on the stems of emergent or floating vegetation. Damselflies are different from dragonflies in certain respects. They are smaller and more delicate, and when they land they hold their wings closed together alongside or over their body. Dragonflies perch with their wings spread. While dragonflies fly above the pond catching mosquitoes and other flying insects, the damselflies glean insects from plant foliage. There are about 500 species of dragonflies in North America, over 100 species in California. Close-focus binoculars will make watching dragonflies, at your own pond or in the wild, even more fun.

Plants for Ponds and Bogs

Native plants offer the most value to wildlife, whether in ponds or on land. Look for locally sourced plants at native plant nurseries, nurseries specializing in wetland or riparian plants, or reputable pond shops. Please do not collect plants from the wild or protected areas such as parks, refuges, and wetlands. (See Appendix I for plant sources.)

*California native plants

Emergent Plants

*Arrowhead (*Sagittaria latifolia*). Small white flowers, beautiful foliage, can grow in water up to two feet in depth

Blue pickerelweed (*Pontederia cordata*). Small blue flowers rise up from heart-shaped leaves

*Cardinal flower (*Lobelia cardinalis*). Red flowers attractive to hummingbirds, also good for bog areas

Cattail (*Typha* spp.). Smaller, non-native species best for backyard ponds; they will need thinning

*Horsetail (*Equisetum* spp.). Aggressive emergent plant, needs to be contained

*Mare's tail (*Hippuris vulgaris*). Ferny foliage, caterpillar host plant for Common Buckeye butterfly

Parrot's feather (*Myriophyllum aquaticum*). Not recommended, very
  aggressive, requires frequent maintenance
*Water plantain (*Alisma plantago-aquatica*). A large-leafed rosette,
  small, white flowers held on upright stems several feet above
  the water

Western blue flag iris (*Iris missouriensis*). Tall stalks with lilac-blue flowers, native to western North America

Floating but Rooted in Soil

*Creeping water primrose (*Ludwigia* spp.). Darners and damselflies lay their eggs in *Ludwigia*, non-native species especially aggressive

* Water clover (*Marsilea oligosporia*). Aquatic clover-like fern

Water lily (*Nymphaea* spp). Non-native, hardy non-tropical species best for backyard ponds, generally needs replacing every year or so

Free-floating Plants

*Duckweed (*Lemna minor*). Tiny fronds shade the water, help reduce algae. *Note:* In most ponds duckweed spreads aggressively; remove excess plants frequently by skimming the pond surface with a net; use surplus in compost piles or as mulch in the garden

*Fairy weed/water fern (*Azolla filiculoides*). Tiny perennial fern with spreading habit, turns reddish-purple in fall; helps reduce algae. *Note:* Also aggressive in ponds and excess plants must be skimmed regularly off the pond surface; use as compost or mulch in the garden

Water hyacinth (*Eichhornia crassipes*). Easily available but not recommended for ponds, very aggressive

Underwater Plants

Underwater plants are oxygenating plants that are nourished directly from the pond water, starving algae in the process.

*Hornwort (*Ceratophyllum demersum*).

Water buttercup (*Ranunculus aquatilis*).

Water purslane (*Didiplis diandra*). Found throughout North America

The shallow beach area at the Biggses' pond allows wildlife to safely approach to bathe and drink.
PHOTOGRAPH BY DAVE BIGGS.

*Waterweed/goldfish plant (*Elodea canadensis*).

Bogs and Pond Edges

Bee balm (*Monarda didyma*). Bushy perennial for bogs, spreads easily, tubular flowers in shades of pink, red and lavender; a favorite of hummingbirds

Bog sage (*Salvia uliginosa*). Airy, upright shrub for bogs, 4–6 feet tall, blue flowers summer through fall, spreads easily by rhizomes

*California gray rush (*Juncus patens*). Stiff, dense gray-green stems about 2 feet tall, grows in bogs and shallow water. *Southern rush (*Juncus acutus*) grows to 6 feet; dark green foliage with sharp, pointed stems

*California polypody (*Polypodium californicum*). Attractive California native fern found along stream banks; plant among rocks at pond edges in shade/filtered sun

*Creek monkeyflower (*Mimulus guttatus*). Bright-yellow tubular flowers in spring/summer are attractive to hummingbirds, compact/taller varieties, reseeds easily

*Indian rhubarb (*Darmera peltata*). Large perennial with huge leaves and clusters of pink flowers on tall stalks in spring, allow room to spread at pond or stream edges

Marsh marigold (*Caltha palustris*). Easy-to-grow bog plant, abundant bright-yellow flowers in spring, attractive to pollinators; native marsh marigold species may be less easily available

*Mugwort (*Artemisia douglasiana*). Distinctive, pleasant scent, silver-gray foliage, butterfly host plant, likes moist places

*Scarlet monkeyflower (*Mimulus cardinalis*). Perennial plant for bogs and other wet areas, tubular, scarlet flowers in summer, bright green foliage, a hummingbird favorite

*Stream sedge (*Carex nudata*). Attractive clumping sedge for pond edges, white-and-yellow flower stalks; also many non-native sedges

Swamp milkweed (*Asclepias incarnata*). Showy, summer-blooming perennial for bogs; butterfly host plant for Monarch

Water hyssop (*Bacopa monnieri*). Forms mat, white to pale blue flowers; plant in pot in pond or at pond edge

*Western five-finger fern (*Adiantum aleuticum*). Small fern with lacy, delicate structure; also non-native *Adiantum* species available

*Yellow-eyed grass (*Sisyrinchium californicum*). Perennial for bogs; grass-like foliage forms clumps, small yellow flowers in spring/summer, to one-foot tall

CHAPTER 5

Front Yard Habitat: Burying the Lawn Aesthetic

On average, homeowners pour from 40 to 60 percent of their household water on lawns, shrubs, and bedding plants.

— Andy Wasowski, *The Landscaping Revolution*

Those large green rectangles that most of us have obediently fed, raked, weeded, and watered at one time or another, have become outdated. Perhaps lawns have outlived their usefulness as a tradition, a symbol of respectability and status brought to this country by early English landowners. The need to take responsibility for conserving water and keeping it clean may be our strongest inducement for burying the lawn aesthetic. The artificial life support that keeps lawns green and growing—chemical fertilizers and toxic garden pesticides and herbicides—kills beneficial insects and harms wildlife. It pollutes our rivers, streams, and bays, carried there by excess water use and storm runoff. Fuel-burning gas mowers and weed-eaters pollute the air with fumes and incessant noise. The combination of water scarcity issues and incentives

Berkeley sedge (*Carex divulsa*) is an attractive lawn alternative.
PHOTOGRAPH BY MICHAEL CREEDMAN.

FACING PAGE: Seasonal nectar flowers, including hollyhocks, sunflowers, and zinnias, combine with kale, chard, and other vegetables in Cindy LaMar's front habitat garden (see Garden Profile, p. 158). PHOTOGRAPH BY CINDY LAMAR.

to replace lawns—from water district rebates to city-run "Cash for Grass" programs—have made the lawn seem an indulgence that we can no longer afford. Even worse, the clipped hedges and lawns of conventional landscapes represent very little value to wildlife. Replacing or reducing the lawn can be an exciting opportunity. So many possibilities open up, each one an attractive alternative that is capable of thriving with minimal water, feeding, and attention. For example:

Native deergrass (*Muhlenbergia rigens*) and *Bidens ferulifolia* mix with other grasses and perennials in this front border. PHOTOGRAPH BY CHARLOTTE TORGOVITSKY.

- A bunchgrass meadow or evergreen groundcover
- An edible landscape or fragrant herb garden
- A mix of trees, shrubs, flowers, and grasses, perhaps set off with a boulder or garden sculpture
- A Mediterranean pollinator garden of fragrant mounds of lavender, catmint, rosemary, and thyme
- A cottage garden of herbs, grasses, and old-fashioned flowers, such as Michaelmas daisy (*Aster novae-angliae*), hollyhocks (*Alcea rosea*), wallflowers (*Erysimum* spp.), Dame's rocket (*Hesperis matronalis*), poppies (*Papaver* spp.), or other heirloom varieties

- A desert scape or succulent garden planted with agave, cacti, aloe, sedum, or desert shrubs such as chuparosa (*Justicia californica*), fairy duster (*Calliandra californica*), or globe mallow (*Sphaeralcea ambigua*)

Unlike the instant overnight fix of a lawn, an aesthetically pleasing natural landscape takes some imagination, research, patience, and, possibly, some professional help. It is a long-term investment and ongoing relationship that deserves careful consideration. The key to replac-

ing a lawn with a more natural California landscape is to select as a replacement a mix of low-water-use plants or grasses that need little maintenance and care. Native plants and other plants adapted to our climate and soils should be the major players. The many beautiful textures and shapes of native bunchgrasses and sedges, for example, make them a good choice for a lawn substitute. From dense and spiky to tall and feathery, native bunchgrasses work well solo or in harmony with native shrubs, wildflowers, or perennials. Mounding combinations of fragrant shrubby Mediterranean perennials mixed with grasses or boulders work beautifully together as stunning front yard habitat, especially for hot,

A diversity of plants, including palo verde, red yucca, sages, and Matilija poppies, transforms this front yard into wildlife habitat. PHOTOGRAPH BY SUSAN GOTTLIEB.

sunny locations. Sage, penstemon, lavender, santolina, and germander (*Teucrium chamaedrys*), for example, combine to provide an attractive low-water and deer-resistant front yard landscape with good wildlife value. Both chaste tree (*Vitex agnus-castus*) with its showy violet flower panicles and strawberry tree (*Arbutus unedo*) are low-water-use plants attractive to butterflies, bees, and birds that are not nibbled by deer. "As soon as someone decides to rip out a lawn," says author and eco-theologian Thomas Berry, "he or she must ask the gardener's questions: What's right for this place? . . . How can I use Nature here without abusing it?"

Getting Rid of the Lawn

Conventional methods of removing lawns depend on the type: a seeded or sod lawn. Sod cutters work on sod lawns, which have a netting underneath; seeded lawns can be dug out or rototilled. However, tilling and hoeing rip apart the layers of soil that house beneficial microorganisms important for plant health. Solarizing the lawn is one method for removing Bermuda grass, a persistent weed grass that is difficult to kill. For this, the lawn is covered with clear plastic and the edges are sealed to keep in the heat. The plastic covering heats up the soil and kills seeds and pathogens through the solarizing effect of the sun's radiation. It is most effective with high temperatures. While it may be an option for small lawns, covering large areas with plastic that must be sealed becomes more difficult. The least desirable method is killing the lawn with herbicides. Consider the potential risks: the toxic chemicals required to achieve this effect will poison the microorganisms important to soil

The Mansurs in San Jose, CA, transformed their front lawn (below) into a Monarch Waystation, filled with native milkweed and nectar plants for butterflies and other pollinators (right) (see Garden Profile, p.136). PHOTOGRAPHS BY HERMINA MANSUR.

health and they will remain in the soil where they may be carried away in garden-water runoff to contaminate waterways and groundwater. It may be expedient, but it carries long-lasting side effects for the health of children, domestic animals, and wildlife, and even the soil.

There is an alternative to conventional methods of removing a lawn that does not require large amounts of plastic or herbicides or rototilling: sheet mulching. Sheet mulching with newspaper or cardboard (best for lawn removal) is a sustainable and effective technique for getting rid of weeds, preparing new planting beds, and for taking out lawns. Sheet mulching may not be a household word, but it is a grassroots phenomenon. It's cheap, easy, and it works. It also does not require fossil fuels. Sheet mulching smothers grass and weeds while leaving the soil undisturbed, and it has the added benefit of enriching the soil in the process. Unlike tilling and hoeing, sheet mulching preserves the top

Sheet Mulching

Sheet mulching smothers weeds and grass without disturbing the structure of the earth underneath or the microorganisms that live in the top layers of the soil. As sheet mulching materials decompose they feed the worms that till the soil. Sheet mulching can be used on bare soil, weedy areas and lawns, and is effective on hardpan and heavy clay soil. No tilling, weeding, herbicides or power equipment is necessary.

1. Cut down weeds or grass, if tall, and water thoroughly. Lay down a thick layer of newspaper (it is easier to spread if wet) or sheets of cardboard. Newspaper is fodder for earthworms, which fertilize and till the soil. Cardboard is best for lawn grasses (use several layers). Overlap newspaper or cardboard sheets to prevent grasses or weeds from coming through. Pay special attention to edges, especially if working with Bermuda grass. (*Optional: Dig a trench around the perimeter of the area to be sheet mulched and pack with rolled up newspaper.*) Bike shops and appliance stores are good sources for cardboard. Be sure to remove staples and tape. For sheet mulching large areas, cardboard can be purchased on a roll from wholesale paper companies. A layer of leaves, manure, or

layers of soil organisms—fungi, microbes, worms, soil bacteria, and other microorganisms—that recycle nutrients, nourish plant roots, and break down organic matter to create healthy soil, which, in turn, helps create healthy plants. Especially effective for heavy clay soils, sheet mulching allows you to plant through the mulch while the vegetation underneath is breaking down. Because Bermuda grass is particularly difficult to get rid of and may reappear, extra layers of cardboard and mulch (an old carpet instead of cardboard is an alternative option for smaller lawn areas) are highly recommended.

compost—whatever is handy—may be used underneath the newspaper or cardboard, if desired. *Optional: Depending on the condition of the soil and/or the intended use for the bed, cover the area with a fine layer of gypsum or oyster shell. Both provide calcium, a necessary nutrient for healthy soil. Gypsum is preferable for clay soils because it helps to improve drainage. If soil is acidic, use oyster shell; if alkaline, choose gypsum. Or sprinkle with rock dust, also known as azomite, for a general source of minerals and trace elements.*

2. Cover newspaper or cardboard with 4-6 inches of mulch: ground-up tree trimmings (arbor chips), soil, leaves, straw (rice straw is weed free), manure, compost, or a combination of organic material. Avoid bark mulch or gorilla hair, which do not decompose. A thick layer of mulch provides nutrients as it decomposes and conserves moisture. As the weeds (or grass) are breaking down, more nutrients are added to the soil as well.

3. Water thoroughly (unless it's raining) and keep watered to the level of the newspaper for four to six weeks. To plant, dig through mulch, adding additional soil or compost if necessary in the planting hole. If newspaper or cardboard is kept moist, it's possible to plant within two or three weeks, especially if the ground is bare.

The following garden profiles illustrate how three owners transformed their lawns into front yard wildlife habitat. The Blackstone Monarch habitat in San Jose, a certified Waystation for the Monarch butterfly, attracts many local butterflies, birds, bees, and other insects. The Pacheco garden in southern California is a mix of native trees, shrubs, perennials, grasses, and annual wildflowers that support a diversity of wildlife. The LaMar-Goerke garden in northern California combines a mix of native and non-native food and nectar plants with edible landscaping.

The Blackstone Monarch Habitat, San Jose, Santa Clara County

As their contribution to Monarch butterfly conservation, Paul and Harmina Mansur designed, constructed, and planted a certified Monarch Waystation on a 6,000 square-foot urban lot that was once mostly lawn. While they were planting milkweed for Monarchs, the Mansurs researched other common butterflies of northern California for caterpillar host plants that might attract local residents. In addition to installing a dominating swath of native milkweed, the owners created drifts of native nectar plants that span the seasons.

Lawn removal: The Mansurs dug out the established sod lawn in the front yard first, including the mesh and several inches of soil underneath. They laid down pieces of recycled concrete as drainage base rock before mounding additional soil, from 6 to 18 inches deep, for raised planting beds. Once the front yard was filled in with butterfly food and nectar plants, the back yard lawn disappeared too—along with the lawn mower! The owners garden organically and never use chemical substances of any kind.

Wildlife focus: Since converting the yard to butterfly habitat the Mansurs have identified fourteen butterfly species in their garden,

including the Monarch, Painted Lady, Acmon Blue, Tailed Copper, Western Tiger Swallowtail, Mourning Cloak, Common Buckeye, Orange Sulphur, and various grass skippers. Many bird species have made this butterfly habitat their home as well, including three species of hummingbirds—Anna's, the year-round resident, and two migrants, the Rufous and Allen's, which have nested in the garden.

A Monarch butterfly is about to emerge from its chrysalis in the Mansurs' wildlife garden. PHOTOGRAPH BY HARMINA MANSUR.

Many birds come to the garden to feed on seeds and insects — Chestnut-backed Chickadees, Cedar Waxwings, Bushtits, Mourning Doves, and numerous others. The owners have also spotted the beautiful White-lined Sphinx moth, which is almost the size of

a hummingbird, and its bright green-and-pink caterpillars on the foliage of the California fuchsia.

Rewards: The Mansurs claim that their butterfly garden has brought in more species of birds, butterflies, bees, and other insects than either of them has seen since their childhoods, and they spend as much time as possible in their garden enjoying the action. They are members of the local chapter of the California Native Plant Society and show their garden on native plant garden tours.

TOP: A Monarch nectars on California buckwheat (*Eriogonum fasciculatum*).
BOTTOM: The Mansurs spotted the caterpillar of the beautiful White-lined Sphinx moth on California fuchsia.
PHOTOGRAPHS BY HARMINA MANSUR.

The Blackstone Monarch Habitat: Partial Plant List of Native Plants

^Butterfly host plants

Trees and Large Shrubs

^California buckeye (*Aesculus californica*) Spring Azure
^Chaparral mallow (*Malacothamnus fasciculatus*) Painted Lady
  and West Coast Lady
Desert willow (*Chilopsis linearis*)
^Hollyleaf cherry (*Prunus ilicifolia*) Pale Swallowtail
^Island mallow (*Lavatera/Malva assurgentiflora*) West Coast Lady,
  Common Checkered Skipper, and Painted Lady
Island snapdragon (*Galvezia speciosa*)
Mock orange (*Philadelphus lewisii*)
^Palmer's bush mallow (*Malacothamnus palmeri*) Painted Lady
Western azalea (*Rhododendron occidentale*)
^Western chokecherry (*Prunus virginiana demissa*) Lorquin's
  Admiral
Western redbud (*Cercis occidentalis*)

Smaller Shrubs

Bush anemone (*Carpenteria californica*)
^Bush monkeyflower (*Mimulus aurantiacus*) Variable Checkerspot
California brittlebush (*Encelia californica*)
^Currant/Gooseberries (*Ribes aureum, R. divaricatum, R. speciosum*)
  Tailed Copper

^Heartleaf keckiella (*Keckiella cordifolia*) Common Buckeye
Sages (*Salvia apiana, S. clevelandii, S. leucophylla, S. mellifera*)
Woolly blue curls (*Trichostema lanatum*)

Perennials

^California aster (*Aster chilensis*) Field Crescent
^California buckwheat (*Eriogonum fasciculatum*) Acmon Blue,
Square-spotted Blue, and Dotted Blue
^California cudweed (*Gnaphalium californicum*) American Lady
California fuchsia (*Epilobium canum*)
California goldenrod (*Solidago californica*)
^California pipevine (*Aristolochia californica*) Pipevine
Swallowtail
California poppy (*Eschscholzia californica*)
^Checkerbloom (*Sidalcea malviflora*) West Coast Lady, Common-
checkered Skipper
Coyote mints (*Monardella macrantha, M. villosa*)
^Deerweed (*Lotus scoparius*) Orange Sulfur, Silvery Blue,
Marine Blue, Acmon Blue, Funereal Duskywing, and other
butterfly species
^Foothill penstemon (*Penstemon heterophyllus*, P. 'Margarita
BOP') Common Buckeye
^Grinnell's beardtongue (*Penstemon grinnellii*) Common Buckeye
^Milkweeds: Showy milkweed (*Asclepias speciosa*), narrow-leaf
milkweed (*A. fasciularis*) Monarch butterfly
Sage (*Salvia spathacea*)

Garden Profile

The Pacheco Wildlife Garden, Fountain Valley, Orange County

Four miles from the coast in southern California, Stephanie and Ed Pacheco's sunny lot was once mostly lawn, front and back. Motivated to conserve water and to create a sanctuary for local wildlife, Stephanie Pacheco started her two-year project by first taking out the front lawn. Piece by piece the lawn was removed and replaced with native plants, choices inspired by her affiliation with the California Native Plant Society and her love of hiking in Nature. Using a catalogue from Tree of Life Nursery, Stephanie checked the size, flowering times, and requirements for each of the plants she chose. Close to 500 California native trees, shrubs, and ground plants gradually replaced two large tracts of Bermuda grass to form a diverse and multi-layered habitat for birds, insects, lizards, and other local wildlife.

Tall, fast-growing, and drought-tolerant fern-leaf ironwoods from the Channel Island plant community provide shade and privacy, and cover and nesting sites for wildlife. Other Channel Island plants—tree ceanothus, island bush poppy, island snapdragon—provide nectar in spring and summer. Native coral bells, endemic to the Channel Islands and attractive to hummingbirds, grow near the shady areas of the house. Layers of sun-loving and drought-tolerant chaparral plants—ceanothus, coffeeberry, manzanita—mingle with understory shrubs of hollyleaf cherry, toyon, and lemonade berry, all offering nectar, berries, and foraging sites for birds, pollinators, and beneficial insects.

Drifts of perennials and annuals open up areas for nectar-collecting bees and butterflies. Wildflowers in spring transition into summer-blooming matilija poppies and native brittlebush followed by California fuchsia and asters in the fall. At least a dozen butterfly host and nectar plants are scattered among the nectar flowers, including California buckwheat, lupine, milkweed, and checkerbloom. Many species of hard-working salvias cover the nectar seasons for hummingbirds, bees, and beneficial insect predators. Noteworthy are the varied levels, shapes, and textures of the grasses and groundcovers—dwarf coyote bush,

In the spring desert apricot mallow (*Sphaeralcea ambigua* 'Louis Hamilton'), lilac verbena (*Verbena lilacina*), bladderpod (*Isomeris arborea*), and California poppies bloom in this front habitat garden. PHOTOGRAPH BY NANCY HEULER.

woodland strawberry, creeping wild rye, deergrass—that tie together the many layers of the understory. The fragrances of pine, pitcher sage, and purple-flowering woolly blue curls enhance the sensory pleasures of this unique wild garden. Habitat at the Pacheco residence also includes a backyard food garden that puts vegetables, herbs, fruit, and berries on the table throughout the seasons. There are ways in which a wild garden differs from gardens that are more tightly pruned and maintained. If allowed, the plants sort themselves out—some plants will dominate, some will reseed, some plants will show up in a more suitable spot. As a habitat gardener, Stephanie has been open to this flow, allowing her wildlife sanctuary to establish naturally with very little manipulation.

Lawn removal: Stephanie started first with the front lawn of Bermuda grass, removing it by hand, "piece by piece," and replacing each section with native plants over a period of two years. She used the same labor-intensive method in the backyard except for one section, which was sheet mulched with eight inches of straw. Within two months she began digging planting holes through the layers. The straw eventually decomposed, adding to the organic content of the soil.

Garden practices: Stephanie composts and mulches with leaves from the site and most of the garden clippings remain on the ground as mulch. Three compost sites contribute fertilizer for the food garden. A rain chain and rain barrel that the owners installed recycle rainwater from the roof for watering plants. Nearby, a three-foot gravel bioswale holds the overflow from the rain barrel on site. A flagstone sidewalk and permeable pathways of decomposed granite are used in the front habitat garden, and stepping stones serve as pathways throughout the backyard habitat.

Wildlife focus: Before native species were planted, the owners saw mostly American Crows and House Sparrows; now the garden is teeming with warblers and flycatchers and many other bird species that feed on seeds as well as the insects the native plants attract. Cooper's Hawks perch in the canopy and migrants, such as the Western Tanager,

occasionally visit. Hummingbird nests have been seen and a pair of Black Phoebes chose to build their nest on a light box mounted on the side of the house! Pacific Chorus frogs breed in a small, preformed pond decorated with several branches that provide access and escape routes for animals. Mosquitoes are controlled with BTi disks. Two pedestal birdbaths connected to solar panels operate as fountains, offering water for bathing and drinking

year-round. They are filled twice a week in summer, less often in winter, and scrubbed out every few months. A myriad of butterfly nectar plants and over 20 caterpillar food plants bring in Pale Swallowtails, Lorquin's Admirals, Checkered Whites, Monarchs, Painted Ladies, and other butterfly species. Tree of Life Nursery's web site was used as a resource for butterfly host plants and food and nectar plants that bloom in different seasons.

Rewards: "Gardening is one of my most rewarding hobbies," says Stephanie, "and my habitat garden brings Nature close to my office window. Looking out over my garden, I might see goldfinches in the birdbath or dragonflies near the little frog pond. I love watching a hummer's mating flight or Bushtits flying through the shrubs looking for insects. All the wildlife—the lizards and the insects, too—add daily joy to my life. Growing native plants instead of water-guzzling lawns and ornamentals is one way to help reduce the tremendous loss of wildlife habitat." Stephanie shares her wildlife garden on garden tours, including tours sponsored by her local chapter of the California Native Plant Society.

FACING PAGE: Stephanie Pacheco uses both open- and closed-bin composting systems to create mulch for her wildlife garden.
THIS PAGE: Woodland strawberry (*Fragaria vesca*) and other groundcovers protect the soil and hold in moisture. Insects visit the flowers and birds enjoy the fruit.
PHOTOGRAPHS BY NANCY HEULER.

The Pacheco Garden: Partial Plant List of Native Plants

^ Butterfly host plant

Trees and Large Shrubs

^Arroyo willow (*Salix lasiolepis*) Lorquin's Admiral, Mourning Cloak, Western Tiger Swallowtail, and other species

Blue elderberry (*Sambucus mexicana*)

^Chaparral mallow (*Malacothamnus fasciculatus*) Painted Lady and West Coast Lady

^Coast live oak (*Quercus agrifolia*) California Sister, Mournful Duskywing, Propertius Duskywing, and various moth species

^Coffeeberry (*Rhamnus californica*) Pale Swallowtail

^False indigo (*Amorpha fruticosa*) California Dogface, Gray Hairstreak, Silver-spotted Skipper

Fern-leaf ironwood (*Lyonothamnus floribundus* var. *aspleniifolius*)

^Hollyleaf cherry (*Prunus ilicifolia*) Pale Swallowtail

Lemonade berry (*Rhus integrifolia*)

Saltbush (*Atriplex lentiformis breweri*)

Toyon (*Heteromeles arbutifolia*)

^Tree ceanothus (*Ceanothus arboreus*) Spring Azure

Smaller Shrubs

^Bladderpod (*Isomeris arborea*) Becker's White

Bush anemone (*Carpenteria californica*)

^Bush monkeyflower (*Mimulus aurantiacus*) Variable Checkerspot

Fairy duster (*Calliandra eriophylla*)

^Fuchsia-flowered gooseberry (*Ribes speciosum*) Tailed Copper

^Indian mallow (*Abutilon palmeri*) Painted Lady and West Coast Lady

Island bush poppy (*Dendromecon harfordii*)
Pitcher sage (*Lepechinia fragrans*)
Sages: *Salvia muelleri, S. coahuilensis, S. leucophylla* 'Pt. Sal',
    S. sonomensis 'Bee's Bliss', *S. apiana*
Woolly blue curls (*Trichostema lanatum*)

Grasses and Groundcovers

Grass skippers, California Ringlet, and several other butterflies
use various grasses and sedges as butterfly host plants.

Beach strawberry (*Fragaria chiloensis*)
Beach suncups (*Camissonia cheiranthifolia*)
^Creeping wild rye (*Leymus triticoides*) Woodland Skipper
Deergrass (*Muhlenbergia rigens*)
Dwarf coyote bush (*Baccharis pilularis* 'Pigeon Point')
^Foothill needlegrass (*Nassella lepida*); purple needlegrass
    (*Nassella pulchra*) California Ringlet
Foothill sedge (*Carex tumulicola*)
Melic grass (*Melica imperfecta*)

Perennials and Annuals

Blue-eyed grass (*Sisyrinchium bellum*)
^Buckwheats (*Eriogonum grande rubescens, E. giganteum, E.
    fasciculatum*) Various "blues" and "coppers" use specific
    buckwheat species as caterpillar host plants
^California aster (*Aster chilensis*) Field Crescent
California brittlebush (*Encelia californica*)
California fuchsia (*Epilobium* spp.)
^Checkerbloom (*Sidalcea malviflora*) West Coast Lady and
    Common-checkered Skipper; the Painted Lady also uses some
    mallows as host plants
Coral bells (*Heuchera maxima*)
Coyote mint (*Monardella villosa*)

^Cudweeds (*Gnaphalium californicum, G. bicolor*) American Lady
Dudleya spp.
Hedge nettle (*Stachys bullata*)
^Lupines (*Lupinus* spp.) Silvery Blue, Arrowhead Blue, Melissa
　　Blue, Boisduval's Blue, West Coast Lady, and other butterfly
　　species
Matilija poppy (*Romneya coulteri*)
^Milkweeds (*Asclepias fascicularis, A. speciosa*) Monarch and Queen
　　butterflies
^Royal penstemon (*Penstemon spectabilis*) *Penstemon* species may be
　　used by the Common Buckeye
Seaside daisy (*Erigeron glaucus* 'Arthur Menzies')
Wallflower (*Erysimum* spp.)
Yarrow (*Achillea millefolium*)

Native Bunchgrasses as Lawn Alternatives

The summer-gold grasslands of our "Golden State" may have inspired our state motto, but they are not the California grasslands that the early European explorers, miners, and settlers traveled through. Before the introduction of annual European grasses and subsequent overgrazing in the 1800s, the grasslands of California's Native Americans were a diverse carpet of perennial bunchgrasses and wildflowers that burst into a riot of color in spring. There were cool season grasses that grew in spring and fall, flowered in early summer and rested in the hottest months. There were warm season grasses that turned green in summer and went dormant in winter. Though European annual grasses have invaded California's major grasslands, remnants of both valley and coastal prairie grasslands exist throughout the state. Numerous native grasses from these two major grasslands are available through native plant nurseries and seed catalogs for use as specimen plants and as groundcover and lawn alternatives. (See Appendix I, Sources of California Native Plants.)

Many native grasses are long lived and easy to grow and maintain.

Red fescue (*Festuca rubra*) and rush (*Juncus effusus, J. patens, J. acutus*) combine to create a beautiful no-mow meadow.
PHOTOGRAPH AND DESIGN BY ALRIE MIDDLEBROOK.

Unlike European annual grasses, native grasses form a permanent groundcover and are drought tolerant. They also offer more protection from fire than naturalized grasses and they are superior as wildlife plants. Combine native grasses with shrubs and perennials, grow them as groundcover or as a lawn substitute, or mix them with bulbs and wildflowers to create a meadow garden. The following grasses, distinct in color and form, are widely used in gardens of all sizes.

- Deergrass (*Muhlenbergia rigens*). This beautiful large bunchgrass has a solid structure, generally 3 x 3 feet with slender, silvery flower stalks that rise several feet above the foliage, usually late in summer. It can be used in full sun or partial shade, dry or moist soil. It is quite drought tolerant and a good choice for a low hedge, for erosion control on steep slopes or hillsides, for large areas, or by itself as a specimen plant. This dense bunchgrass serves as a substitute for invasive pampas grass and mixes easily with native shrubs and perennials, as well as other Mediterranean-climate plants. Dormant in winter, deergrass displays new growth in

spring. Despite its name, deer do not eat this bunchgrass, but they do like to bed down in it.

- The fescues (*Festuca* spp.). Idaho fescue (*Festuca idahoensis*), California fescue (*F. californica*), and red fescue (*F. rubra*). Of all the native grasses, red fescue is probably the most widely planted as a lawn substitute. A cool-season grass that spreads by rhizomes, red fescue turns from bluish-green to golden in summer. It can be mowed, requires very little water in summer, and tolerates shade. Red fescue 'Molate' is drought tolerant and especially popular as a groundcover. Idaho fescue, with its blue to gray-green color and fine texture, is considered one of the most "ornamental" of the native grasses. This fescue adapts well to most soils, takes full sun or part shade, and tolerates more summer heat than red fescue, though both grasses mix well together. This cool season grass, which grows from one to two feet tall, should not be watered when dormant in the summer. Growing from two to three feet tall, California fescue boasts striking seed wands, which ripen in early summer, that wave above the clumps of green to blue-green foliage. This fescue is ideal for planting under oaks or other dry shady areas, and an excellent choice for steep slopes for erosion control. Native grasses provide cover, foraging sites and nesting materials for birds. Ladybird beetles, too, love to congregate on the native fescues and other bunchgrasses. Many of the grasses also serve as butterfly host plants for the grass skippers and other butterflies.

- Needlegrass (*Nassella* spp.). Purple needlegrass (*Nassella pulchra*), foothill needlegrass (*N. lepida*), and nodding needlegrass (*N. cernua*). The signature plant of valley grasslands, needlegrass is named for its needle-like awns. It is the ideal grass for dry, sunny areas, but it also adapts to moist soils, heat, and drought. Interplant needlegrass with native wildflowers or bulbs for a beautiful meadow. Naturally summer dormant, it should not be watered (or fertilized) during the dry season. Purple needlegrass (three to four feet tall) shows blue-green foliage and purple seed heads in

Wildflowers (*Clarkia unguiculata*, *Gilia capitata*, California poppies), planted from seed, are blooming in May in this small red fescue meadow garden. PHOTOGRAPH AND DESIGN BY ALRIE MIDDLEBROOK.

Meadow Gardens

It is possible to have the green, spacious look of a lawn, John Greenlee points out in his book, *The American Meadow Garden*, by combining a diversity of grasses with annual and perennial nectar flowers that feed pollinators and beneficial insects. The rich color, scents, and textures of meadow gardens, Greenlee reminds us, are reminiscent of wild places—fields or woods or creeks—where we may have spent time as children or places where we have walked or hiked as adults. Meadow gardens require less maintenance than traditional lawns and much fewer resources to sustain them. Greenlee defines meadows as dominated by grasses but with accents of color and texture from bulbs, annuals and perennials. Best of all, meadow gardens do not require large expanses of land. Bulbs and wildflowers—native onion (*Allium* spp.), brodiaeas, lilies, California poppy (*Eschscholzia californica*), blue dicks (*Dichelostemma capitatum*), low-growing lupine, and numerous others—are natural companions to native bunchgrasses and sedges. They also enhance the wildlife value and seasonal beauty. Grasses, of course, don't need wildflowers to succeed, but wildflowers need grasses to protect them from weeds. A front yard (or backyard) prairie meadow can be a challenge to establish, but buying local wildflower seed or bulbs, preparing the ground carefully and controlling weeds increase your chances of success. Wildflowers, wherever they are intended to grow, are best sown in the rainy season, generally November through January.

Low-growing California meadow sedge (*Carex pansa*), planted with California gray rush (*Juncus patens*) and Pacific coast iris (*Iris douglasiana*) turns this yard into a small meadow. PHOTOGRAPH AND DESIGN BY ALRIE MIDDLEBROOK.

spring, then turns gold in summer; the purple awns at the top of the seed stalks make a quirky 90-degree angle. This native grass is adept at colonizing in very poor soil. Drought-tolerant bunchgrasses and native salvias make good companions and they are deer-proof habitat for front yard (and backyard) gardens.

Low-growing Lawn Substitutes

For low-growing lawn alternatives that stay green all year, consider planting drought-tolerant sedges or two low-growing prairie grasses that are popular lawn replacements throughout the West.

- California meadow sedge (*Carex pansa*). This low-growing native sedge from the coastal prairie grassland has a lush, undulating look

and stays green all year with very little water. Though it needs no mowing, it can be trimmed back if needed. Tough, low-maintenance, and able to withstand foot traffic, this versatile groundcover needs minimal water to stay green. It takes sun or shade, clay or sandy soils. Plugs are available at most native plant nurseries.

- Berkeley sedge (*Carex divulsa*). This extremely versatile sedge makes an attractive lawn alternative or mounding ground cover. At 12-18 inches high, Berkeley sedge takes sun or shade, accepts garden water but is drought tolerant. This sedge is not fussy about soil and stays green year-round (in hot areas it may need some water to look its best). Native foothill sedge (*Carex tumulicola*) is similar in appearance but not as vigorous or as showy.
- Buffalo grass (*Buchloe dactyloides*) and blue gramma (*Bouteloua gracilis*). Both of these low-growing prairie grasses are warm-season grasses that turn soft yellow in winter. They take foot traffic, need very little water (and no fertilizer), and can be mowed. Often mixed together in meadow plantings, both grasses are suitable for dry, hot, sunny areas. Blue gramma, which is native to many areas of the country, makes a stunning, easy-to-care-for lawn. Plant in full sun in well-drained soil; do not water in summer. Without occasional mowing, fluffy buffalo grass will spread with runners along the surface, though its roots are not invasive.

Groundcovers as Lawn Alternatives

Groundcover options run the gamut from grasses to the thick cover of low-mounding shrubs. They act as a barrier to weeds, keep the ground cool and moist, and offer shelter and foraging sites to birds and other wildlife. Ideal for small areas or for spaces between pavers, aromatic, low-growing herbs do double duty as groundcovers and nectar plants for pollinators. Herbs that form flat green mats—creeping thyme, caraway-scented thyme, and camphor thyme, English chamomile, woolly yarrow—require minimal water and can take some foot traffic. Butterflies flock to the tiny pink flowers of lippia (*Lippia nodiflora* or *Phyla nodiflora*),

Many native bunchgrasses make attractive lawn substitutes. Pictured here are two lawns planted with Idaho fescue (*Festuca idahoensis*). PHOTOGRAPHS AND DESIGN BY ALRIE MIDDLEBROOK.

Low-growing forms of native shrubs, such as coyote bush (*Baccharis pilularis* 'Twin Peaks' and 'Pigeon Point'), double as groundcover and foraging sites for birds and insects. PHOTOGRAPH BY SUSAN GOTTLIEB.

a low-growing perennial herb found in California and elsewhere in North America. (The species *Phyla nodiflora* var. *nodiflora* is endemic to California alone.) This easy-to-grow groundcover and member of the verbena family goes dormant in winter and spreads across the ground readily as a soft green mat. In the wild, lippia is most often found in moist places but shows up in dry areas as well. If planted in part shade in the garden, lippia would require less water.

Though not amenable to foot traffic, low-growing woody shrubs are a good option for vigorous groundcover, especially on slopes and hillside lots. *Rosmarinus* 'Irene', a hardy and mounding low-growing rosemary, blooms with dark blue nectar flowers in spring (and may bloom in almost any season) and adapts well to dry, sunny sites and micro-climates that experience frost and hard freezes. Our California aster (*Aster chilensis* 'Pt. St. George') forms a low-growing dense mat that blooms in the fall with lavender nectar flowers very attractive to bees and butterflies. Commonly planted Santa Barbara daisy (*Erigeron karvinskianus*), a non-native alternative, also performs well as a ground cover and it's almost always in bloom. Germander (*Teucrium chamaedrys*) forms a dense, drought-tolerant, and deer-resistant low hedge that offers cover and foraging for birds and insects ('Prostratum' grows from four to six inches high). For dry, sunny areas with good drainage, low-growing Sonoma sage (*Salvia sonomensis*) forms a creeping mat of gray-green foliage that blooms in late spring with tiny lavender nectar flowers. One of our most versatile native salvias, hummingbird sage (*Salvia spathacea*) spreads by rhizomes, forming a dark green, clumping groundcover under trees or other small areas. Fuchsia-colored flowers on tall stalks rise above the large, coarse, and sticky leaves that seem especially attractive to hummers, but very uninviting to deer. Hummingbird sage works in dry and moist garden areas and though it can take full sun, this sage is happiest in part shade. Prostrate forms of native shrubs—ceanothus, coyote bush, manzanita—are widely used as groundcover, especially on slopes and large areas. Use native wild ginger (*Asarum caudatum*), noted for its lovely heart-shaped leaves and spicy scent, as a lush groundcover for shady, moist areas or streamside plantings.

Edible Landscaping: Grow Something for the Table

There is something wonderfully satisfying in harvesting vegetables and herbs we've grown from seeds sown in spring or autumn. The convenience of stepping out the door to pick an apple or plum or sprigs of herbs to season a sauce or a bunch of greens for the salad partly explains why food gardens and edible landscaping have become popular once again. In recent years, surging interest in the Slow Food movement, which promotes locally grown food, has led to a revival in vegetable gardening. No longer relegated to the farthest corner of the backyard, food gardens have not only replaced the backyard lawn, they are also turning up in front yards. Growing something for the table is compatible with growing for wildlife—just be prepared to share.

Herbs as multipurpose plants for people and for wildlife are in a category all their own. They are feeding grounds for pollinators. Even if I didn't love the licorice flavor of its leaves in my tea, I would want anise

hyssop (*Agastache foeniculum*) in my garden just for its whimsical beauty. All parts of this graceful plant point upwards, from the small soft purple spikes to the tips of the dark-green, heart-shaped leaves. Mixed with the leaves of lemon verbena, anise hyssop makes a delicious "sun tea" and its flowers are loved by bees and butterflies. Although English chamomile, a feathery plant with small white daisy-like flowers, is especially pretty around stepping stones or along paths in sunny gardens, the German

chamomile makes a better tea. Pick the flowers when the yellow centers are high. Spearmint, peppermint, and other culinary mints are best planted in containers, as they can be quite invasive. Let them flower for the tiny pollinating wasps and flies. All parts of the nasturtium plant—leaves, seedpods, and flowers—are edible, and it serves as a host plant for the Cabbage White butterfly. Hummingbirds nectar on nasturtium and its carefree habit works well as groundcover or spilling over walls or pots.

Surround the tomatoes, cucumbers, and beans with insectary plants—the umbellifers (carrot family members), mints, and other herbs—as beacons for beneficial insects. Cow parsnip, angelica, dill, parsley, culinary fennel, and other umbellifers are also host plants for the Anise Swallowtail. Or plant herbs between pavers and along pathways and at the edges of flowerbeds. One of my favorite herbs is comfrey, though it spreads vigorously and needs space. The flowers in spring attract hummingbirds and bees and the large coarse leaves can be harvested for mulch or compost piles. When added to worm bins, comfrey increases worm reproduction rates. Herbs, the plants that give so much, are, in fact, some of the easiest plants to grow. Browse seed catalogs for herbs, old-fashioned field flowers, and other traditional summer annuals to attract beneficial insects to your food garden from spring through fall. If you grow roses, plant nectar flowers underneath. The beneficial insects they attract will protect the roses and hide those leggy bare stems at the same time. *Tip:* Grow seeds for edibles and flowers in recycled paper coffee cups. Punch a few holes in the bottom, fill them with potting soil, and add seeds. When the plants are large enough for transplanting, remove the bottom, slit the sides, and plant the seed container directly into the ground. The cup gradually decomposes, sparing the plant from transplant shock and you the extra step.

Garden designer Maile Arnold replaced a backyard lawn in Rohnert Park, CA, with raised vegetable beds. Calendulas, interplanted with the veggies, bring in beneficial insects.
PHOTOGRAPH BY NANCY BAUER.

The LaMar-Goerke Wildlife Garden, Mill Valley, Marin County

In 2004 Cindy LaMar, with husband Jon's enthusiastic support and labor, turned a small, level front yard on a hillside lot in Mill Valley into a mini-wildlife sanctuary. The owners converted a lawn into raised beds edged in fieldstone, curving mulched pathways, and a rose-covered arbor. Benches placed in hidden alcoves for enjoying the garden, and the long-distance views, completed the transformation. At one end of the oval-shaped yard Cindy grouped four large shrubs—blue elderberry, manzanita, coffeeberry, and strawberry tree. This cluster of shrubs provides nectar for hummingbirds, bees, and other pollinators in the spring and berries in the fall. California wild grape, which climbs to the second-story balcony, and pink-flowering currant espaliered against the front stairway make good use of vertical space. When the leaves of the wild grape turn scarlet in autumn, Hermit Thrushes and American Robins flock to the vine for its abundant fruit.

Combining mostly annuals and edibles, the center bed is a focal point of riotous color, butterflies, and bees from spring through fall. Composites—sunflowers, cosmos, zinnias, asters—mingle with snapdragons, blue flax, mustard, kale, and chard.

In the fall, Lesser Goldfinches, House Finches, and Titmice feast for months on the seeds of the sunflowers and the tall seed wands of the mustard plants. California and Spotted Towhees scratch in the soil for excess fallen seeds. Around the edges of the garden, perennial flowerbeds of mostly Mediterranean nectar plants include sages (for fragrance and nectar for bees and hummers), verbenas (for butterflies), and catmints (as bee magnets and for their long bloom period). Scattered throughout the garden are multiple bathing and drinking options—a pedestal birdbath, a large shallow concrete bowl, a pottery saucer on a tree stump, and a large hollowed-out rock.

The center front bed, which changes each spring, includes hollyhocks, clarkia, sunflowers, cosmos, kale, mustard greens, and other edibles. Goldfinches mine the seed wands of mustard for months.
PHOTOGRAPH BY CINDY LAMAR.

Lawn removal: The owners used Toby Hemenway's sheet mulching technique, described in his book on permaculture (*Gaia's Garden*), to remove the lawn. They watered the lawn first, and then opened it up (without turning the soil) with a spading fork. Next, they marked out the flowerbeds, edged them in rock, and laid down tightly overlapped sheets of cardboard on top of a layer of horse manure. Additional layers of manure, compost and straw were laid on top of the wet cardboard to a depth of almost two feet. Cardboard and path mulch covered what remained of the lawn as pathways. Cindy picked up heavy-duty cardboard boxes at a large appliance store and the manure was free at a local stable. The flowerbeds were well watered until the rains began a month later in November and were ready for planting the following March. Sheet mulching materials and recipes differ; only a few essentials are critical. "As long as you have enough cardboard or newspaper plus organic material of any kind," says Hemenway, "you'll end up with great soil." *One caveat*: Straw is a good mulch option, but not hay, which contains seeds of weedy plants.

Garden practices: Cindy feeds the soil with compost once or twice a year and plant trimmings are tucked under shrubs as mulch. No pesticides or synthetic fertilizers are used. "When you poison insects, weeds, or rodents," says Cindy, "you also poison whatever eats them." By pruning and cleaning up only once a year, in February, Cindy maintains cover and plenty of foraging opportunities for birds (seeds, insects, and fruit) and other creatures. Inline drip irrigation connects the raised beds to different irrigation valves for various watering needs during the dry season, which allows for a conservative watering schedule. The owners update the controller schedule regularly, based on the weather and season. Birdbaths are filled daily with fresh water and scrubbed out as needed.

Wildlife focus: Forty–two species of birds have been counted since the lawn was replaced; seven species have nested somewhere in the garden. Bewick's Wrens, Chestnut-backed Chickadees, and Oak Titmice have chosen nest boxes; California Towhees nest in the bushes and Bushtits, Anna's Hummingbirds, and Great Horned Owls nest in the

pines in the back yard. California Quail, frequently in a covey of 20 at a time, visit the garden on a regular basis, foraging and taking dust baths in spots where soil is exposed. Shy Hermit Thrushes and the striking black-and-yellow Townsend's Warblers are frequent visitors. Plentiful butterfly nectar plants and caterpillar host plants attract local butterflies, including the Pale Swallowtail, whose caterpillars have been found on the coffeeberry, one of its caterpillar food plants. Beneficial insect predators—garden spiders, soldier beetles, and ladybird beetles—are often spotted in the garden.

Rewards: "I was inspired to create this garden to provide food and shelter for wildlife," says Cindy, "and in return it rewards me with a wonderful place to appreciate Nature right outside my door. I am amazed at the amount of bird and insect life all around us, and I love to sit in the garden, inhaling all the sweet and spicy flower scents and watching what goes on. It often seems almost magical." Cindy had the garden certified as wildlife habitat from the National Wildlife Federation in 2005 and her garden was featured on Marin's Eco-Friendly Garden Tour in 2010.

In the fall Hermit Thrushes and American Robins feed on the fruit of California wild grape (*Vitis californica* 'Roger's Red') that climbs to the second story balcony.
PHOTOGRAPH BY CINDY LAMAR.

LaMar-Goerke Garden: Partial Plant List from Front Yard Habitat

*California native plants
^ Butterfly host plant

Trees and Shrubs

*Blue elderberry (*Sambucus mexicana*)
Butterfly bush (*Buddleia davidii*)
^*California lilacs (*Ceanothus* 'Concha', *C. thyrsiflorus* 'Skylark')
   Spring Azure, California Tortoiseshell, California Hairstreak,
   Hedgerow Hairstreak; Ceanothus Silk moth, Common Sheep
   moth
^*Coffeeberry (*Rhamnus californica*) Gray Hairstreak and Pale
   Swallowtail
Flowering maple (*Abutilon* 'Victor Reitor')
*Manzanita (*Arctostaphylos* 'Louis Edmunds')
^*Pink-flowering currant (*Ribes sanguineum* var. *glutinosum*)
   Tailed Copper
Sages (*Salvia clevelandii*, **S. apiana*, *S. buchananii*, *S. canariensis*,
   S. guaranitica for spring bloom; *S. coccinea* 'Brenthurst',
   S. microphylla 'Rosita', *S. sclarea*, *S. verticillata* for summer
   bloom; *S. elegans*, *S. mexicana* 'Limelight' for late summer/fall
   bloom; *S. gesneriflora* 'Tequila' for winter bloom)
Strawberry tree (*Arbutus unedo*)

Perennials and Vines

*California fuchsia (*Epilobium* spp.)
*California wild grape (*Vitis californica* 'Roger's Red')
Catmint (*Nepeta racemosa* 'Walker's Low')
^*Checkerbloom (*Sidalcea malviflora*) West Coast Lady, Painted

Lady, and Common-checkered Skipper

Cleome (*Cleome* 'Sparkler Lavender') — birds love the seeds

Coreopsis spp.

Cosmos bipinnatus

Germanders (*Teucrium chamaedrys*, *T. majoricum*)

^Milkweed (*Asclepias curassavica*) Monarch

^Passion vine (*Passiflora caerulea*) Gulf Fritillary

^*Penstemon heterophyllus* 'Blue Springs' Common Buckeye

Purple coneflower (*Echinacea purpurea*)

*Seaside daisy (*Erigeron glaucus*)

Sedum telephium 'Autumn Joy'

Sunflowers (*Helianthus angustifolius*, *H. annuus*)

^Toadflax (*Linaria purpurea*) Common Buckeye

Thyme (*Thymus* spp.)

Verbenas (*Verbena bonariensis*, *V. lilacina* 'De La Mina')

Zinnia spp.

*Spring-blooming wildflowers: Baby blue eyes (*Nemophila menziesii*), California poppy (*Eschscholzia californica*), Chinese houses (*Collinsia heterophylla*), globe gilia (*Gilia capitata*), tidy tips (*Layia platyglossa*)

^*Grasses and Sedges*

*Foothill sedge (*Carex tumulicola*), Crinkled hairgrass (*Deschampsia flexuosa*), *Idaho fescue (*Festuca idahoensis* 'Siskiyou Blue'). Grasses and sedges are butterfly host plants for grass skippers and other butterflies

Plant Combinations for Pots

Whether large shallow containers, wine half-barrels or something in-between, pots expand our gardening options, whether it's kids and animals, gophers, or just not enough planting space that's the issue. Most wildflower species and many native bulbs, such as wild onion (*Allium* spp.), *Brodiaea* spp., fairy lan-

terns, and mariposa lilies (*Calochortus* spp.), are candidates for the large shallow containers. There are almost endless combinations of perennials, small shrubs, grasses, and succulents that would make stunning and valuable wildlife displays for larger pots. Mix different plant forms together—a grass, a small shrub or perennial, a trailing plant. Consider wildlife value, seasonal bloom, and striking color combinations.

For example:

- Sow wildflower seed in a large shallow bowl. Try baby blue eyes (*Nemophila menziesii*), tidy tips (*Layia platyglossa*), bird's-eye gilia (*Gilia tricolor*), Chinese houses (*Collinsia heterophylla*), or one of the clarkia species, by themselves or in combination.

- For large shallow bowls or larger pots, mix one of the smaller native buckwheats (*Eriogonum grande rubescens* or *E. latifolium*) and coast rockcress (*Arabis blepharophylla*) with blue-eyed grass (*Sisyrinchium bellum*) and dudleyas or other succulents.

- Mix a shrub such as fairy duster bush (*Calliandra eriophylla*) or bush monkeyflower (*Mimulus aurantiacus* or hybrids) or any of the smaller sages (*Salvia coccinea, S. microphylla, S. nemerosa, S. patens*) with grasses or sedges to feed hummingbirds. Idaho fescue (*Festuca idahoensis*), foothill sedge (*Carex tumulicola*), and *Carex* 'Frosty Curls' are good choices for pot combinations.

- Combine old-fashioned, summer-blooming nectar flowers such as plains coreopsis (*Coreopsis tinctoria*), zinnia, or black-eyed Susan (*Rudbeckia hirta*) with butterfly host plants—tropical milkweed (*Asclepias curassavica*) for Monarchs, snapdragons or toadflax for the Buckeye butterfly, or checkerbloom (*Sidalcea malviflora*) for the West Coast Lady (at least three of each host plant).

- Culinary herbs—thyme, oregano, marjoram, lavender, culinary sage, mints—are ideal candidates for pot habitat for bees and other pollinators.

A pot filled with ornamental grasses and Mexican marigold (*Tagetes lemonii*) highlights a meadow of California fescue (*Festuca californica*). PHOTOGRAPH AND DESIGN BY ALRIE MIDDLEBROOK.

Spring-blooming shrubs mix with summer-blooming zinnias, hollyhocks, daisies, and sunflowers to provide cover, food, and nectar in this wildlife habitat garden. PHOTOGRAPH BY CINDY LAMAR.

Starting a Habitat Garden

rowing a wildlife habitat garden does not need to be expensive or difficult. Little by little any garden can be made more wildlife-friendly. Take a walk through your own plot. What habitat essentials — cover, food and nectar plants, water — are you providing right now? Are there fences or trellises available for vines that produce nectar for hummingbirds or fruit for birds? Are there plants that have little wildlife value that could be gradually replaced with trees, shrubs, or ground plants that provide nectar flowers or food and cover for birds? Take an inventory of plants to determine what native plants already exist on site and which non-native plants you want to preserve; then consider which available food and nectar plants will have the most impact in your garden. A plant screen of berry-producing shrubs might not only serve wildlife but also give more privacy from neighbors or cars. Is there a place for a birdbath? For drifts of seasonal nectar flowers? Which host plants for local butterflies could you add near the nectar flowers? Take a look, too, at traffic patterns in the garden; you may want to focus first on improving the wildlife value of those areas of the garden where foot traffic and human activity is lightest.

When a gardener decides to plant for wildlife, a new relationship with the land evolves, a new mindset takes hold. The garden is no longer outdoor decoration; it becomes a web of life, a thriving mini-ecosystem, a sanctuary for songbirds, bees, butterflies, and numerous other creatures. Because wildlife gardens try to imitate Nature, they become diverse and fascinating places in any season, and a daily invitation to experience adventure, pleasure, and joy.

What we do with our piece of the planet and what we do collectively to increase biodiversity counts now more than ever. Whether we choose to plant wildlife gardens, fight invasive plants, restore creeks, or plant a school butterfly garden, we can choose to make a difference, at our own pace in our own way. When habitat restoration spreads from one garden to another, from one neighborhood to another — when towns, such as Alpine, California, become certified as wildlife habitats — new wildlife corridors are created that facilitate the movement and nourishment of wildlife species, helping to both alleviate the negative impacts of habitat loss and prevent the loss of more species. Habitat gardens can also serve as useful educational tools for children — and adults — that teach how we, as keystone species, play an increasingly vital role in protecting our wildlife, our watersheds, and our own health and well-being.

And don't forget to expect the unexpected!
PHOTOGRAPH BY MIEKO WATKINS.

167

APPENDIX A

Natural Gardening Guidelines

Garden with a sense of place. We Californians live in a Mediterranean climate region—cool wet winters, warm dry summers. The plants most adapted to our climate are California's native plants and plants from other Mediterranean climate regions. From this huge plant palette comes a great diversity of beautiful, easy-to-grow, low-water-use plants that feed and shelter birds, insects, and other wildlife.

Choose the right plant for the right place. It may seem a simple suggestion but if professional and home gardeners practiced it faithfully, most plant problems would probably vanish. Group plants according to their needs for dry sunny places or wet sunny places, dry shade or wet shade. Honor the integrity of a plant by allowing it to grow in a space that will accommodate its mature size.

Know the watering needs of plants. Check garden books, local nurseries, and plant websites for watering guidelines. Regularly walk the garden, poke a finger in the ground, and look at your plants. Plants are alive and, like us, have needs that change from season to season. Most gardeners overwater plants, whether they require moderate amounts of water or very little. Plants may not be able to live without water, but they also can be killed by root rot from too much. Mediterranean-climate plants, including most of our natives, are adapted to dry summers. If you use an irrigation system, watering schedules and run-times should be available from your local water company. It pays to personally oversee the irrigation system and supervise hired gardeners, who are prone to overwatering. Make sure the irrigation system is designed to water the soil, not the plant. When irrigation is set up for individual plants, the space between dries out, preventing healthy root development. Improve drainage by creating raised beds or mounds and save on water by planting small, water-conserving shrubs and mounding perennials close together, which allows them to lock in moisture as they cover the ground.

Grow healthy soil. The soil is where it all begins and ends, from birthing the seedling to embracing the decaying leaf, petal, and twig. "Feed the soil, not the plant" is the mantra of all successful gardeners, and all you need for healthy soil is compost and mulch. Organic matter provides a beneficial environment for the microorganisms and fungi that are so beneficial for plant growth. Releasing its nutrients slowly into the soil, organic matter also feeds the earthworms so they can do their hard work of tilling and re-tilling the soil, offering their castings as fertilizer in the process.

Pull weeds before they go to seed and tuck them under shrubs where they will enrich the soil as they decompose, or add them to compost piles or small brush piles in the back corners of the garden. Leaves are garden gold and they are free. Sadly, they too often get bagged and hauled away. Leaves, pulled weeds, and garden trimmings placed on garden beds decompose quickly and can be turned into the soil as you plant. As they break down, their stored nutrients are released back into the earth as humus—Nature's very own process. A top dressing of mulch holds in moisture, provides a layer of insulation, and cuts down on water use in the summer. Always keep mulch away from trunks, root crowns, and stems of plants.

Organic mulch includes chopped-up plant trimmings, leaf mulch, decomposed compost, straw, woodchips, and bark. Bark mulch and gorilla hair are often used as a weed barrier; however, neither nourishes the soil nor provides nesting places for bees and other insects. Gorilla hair also acts as a water barrier. Heavy mulching of any type discourages groundnesting native bees. Try to leave some soil bare, or lightly covered in leaves, in undisturbed areas of the garden away from foot traffic to provide nesting areas. *Note:* Native plants do not need rich soil, fertilizers, or heavy mulch; instead, allow the plant's own leaf litter to remain as mulch. Plants from desert, coastal scrub, and chaparral, for example, thrive on slopes and bluffs in dry, lean, often rocky soil with good drainage. Small rocks could be used as mulch, but avoid organic mulch, which would hold in moisture and potentially rot the plants. Drainage can be improved by planting on raised beds, berms, or mounds. Natives from forest plant communities, however, that grow in thick leaf mulch are more accepting of garden mulch.

Prune lightly and judiciously. Low-impact pruning protects butterfly caterpillars and chrysalides that hide among leaves, twigs, and branches. Deadhead flowers enough to encourage new growth, but allow plants, especially composites (sunflower family), to go to seed in late summer and fall to feed finches and other seed-eating birds. Allow hedges and hedgerows to grow into their natural form and height, to flower and set fruit to provide cover and food for birds and other wildlife. Strive for a more informal, less tidy look.

Plant native plants in late fall or winter. Spring may be the season that stirs a gardener's soul, but fall is the best time to plant. Young trees, shrubs, and perennials have a chance to become established while the soil is still warm. Planting in late fall to take advantage of winter rains is best for natives, which must grow long roots for the dry months ahead. When planting native trees and shrubs, dig a generous hole and disturb the root ball as little as possible. Gently loosen roots or cut severely pot-bound roots. Do not add amendments or fertilizers, just native soil. Water very thoroughly. Always avoid watering near the crown of the plant. Remember that drought-tolerant plants need water to get established.

Buy small plants that are not in bloom. Smaller plants will catch up with and often surpass the larger ones that have been in the pot for a long time. Check to make sure plants are not root bound (roots coming out of the bottom). Well-fertilized nursery plants that have been watered to encourage lush growth look very appealing to deer. Even deer-tolerant plants fresh from the nursery

Robins and other bird species forage for insects and seeds in garden mulch and plant debris.
PHOTOGRAPH BY ROBERT WATKINS.

are vulnerable. They may need to be protected a season or two with cages or nets. *Hint:* For an effective deer-repellent spray, mix 16 ounces of water with two eggs and a dash of cooking oil. Spray the plant weekly and after each rainfall.

Avoid the use of synthetic fertilizers, pesticides, and herbicides. A combination of healthy soil with regionally appropriate plants in the right place helps prevent weak and unhealthy plants, which are more vulnerable to insect damage. High-nitrogen fertilizers accelerate leafy, vulnerable growth that attracts leaf-chewing insects. Pesticides not only kill the insects that feed insect predators but also kill the beneficial insects, and they contaminate the nectar flowers that beneficial insects and hummingbirds feed on. Garden chemicals pollute our ground water and eventually find their way to local waterways. By gardening organically, we help protect the health of our watersheds. If you must use any toxic or pesticide alternative, spot treat only. The least toxic alternatives include Safer's soap, Neem, dormant oils, and soaps. Generally, manual methods, such as spraying foliage with water, are just as effective.

Use natural materials for pathways and walkways. Keep water on the land by using porous materials that absorb water—path mulch (chipped or shredded wood waste, wood chips, and shavings), bricks, flagstones set on sand, decomposed granite, gravel—for pathways and walkways. Paths of porous materials act like a sponge and hold the water on the landscape. Non-permeable materials allow heavier and faster runoff to creeks, which erodes creek beds and edges. Asphalt and concrete surfaces, for example, allow water to run off quickly, which picks up oil residues from cars and other pollutants as it makes its way to storm drains. Create natural pathways with whatever plant materials are at hand. Leaf litter and petals and chopped up plant trimmings are soft to walk on and absorb rain. Save newspapers for sheet mulching weedy areas and new planting beds. Almost everything can be used again in a different form or to create something new. Use recycled materials for building walls and decks, for making paths, and for creating garden artwork and planting beds.

Plant Propagation Tips

(Courtesy of Charlotte Torgovitsky; see Charlotte's Garden in Ch. 3.)

Seeds are food for many creatures and are also necessary to ensure the survival of a plant species. Always get permission first if you are collecting seeds beyond your own garden. Even in your own garden, collect sparingly and over a period of days or weeks and, if possible, from several different plants of the same species. Collect seeds during dry weather or in the afternoon; moist seeds are vulnerable to molds. Do not store freshly collected seed in a plastic bag or closed jar; open plastic food containers or paper envelopes are better options. Allow seeds to dry thoroughly (generally two or three weeks), then clean seeds with a sieve or winnow off plant debris. When seeds are cleaned and dried, store in jars or envelopes in a cool, dark, and dry place.

Always label your seed; don't rely on memory or visual clues (flower head, leaf, or stem), which can sometimes be confusing.

One of the most common mistakes made with seeds is to bury them too deeply. Very fine seed (*Mimulus* spp., for example) simply needs to be tamped down into the soil medium. Small seed (*Salvia* spp.) should be tamped into the medium, and then lightly covered with perlite, pumice or vermiculite. Larger seed (*Lupinus* spp.) can be buried in the soil medium, covered with more medium, and then tamped solidly. Rule of thumb: bury seed no more than the diameter of the seed. Propagating plants from seeds requires daily attention, especially in the early stages right after germination. Keeping the soil medium moist is critical to good root development, which in turn grows a strong plant.

To germinate the seeds of many California perennials, prepare the seed flats or trays in late summer or early fall. This method mimics a natural *stratification* process that exposes the seeds to changing day length, falling temperatures, and rainfall. Make sure the medium is moist, and then carefully sow seeds and water gently. Cover the seed flat with cloud-cover fabric to protect against predators. Place the flat outdoors in a protected, shady spot where it will get moisture once the rains start. Some seeds will take months to germinate. Once germination starts, loosen the fabric cover and water the seedlings regularly. Transplant when the first set of true leaves has formed.

There are other ways for a propagator to simulate the stratification process. The seeds of summer annuals are affected by changing temperatures and day lengths, and must sense a certain minimum moisture level before germinating. Many perennial plants from higher altitudes need to experience a winter chill first; the germination process will begin, but active growth won't occur until the days get warmer and longer. Some seeds need to "ripen" once they've been dropped from the parent plant; the propagator helps this process along by drying and cleaning the seeds.

Depending on the species, one or more of the following treatments may help improve germination.

- Soak the seed in hot water
- Mix seed with a moistened medium; refrigerate for two to three months. Be sure to label seed. Keep it moist and aerate the medium by checking on it regularly. As soon as you notice germination, pot in soil mix.
- A Gro-light set for 12 to 14 hours a day fools some seeds into thinking it's spring. Some seeds need light and cool soil; other seeds respond to light and a warm, moist soil. A propagation mat, with seedling flats elevated about one inch above it, brings the soil temperature to about 70 degrees, which promotes germination in many annuals and some common perennial plants such as coneflower (*Echinacea purpurea*) and deergrass (*Muhlenbergia rigens*).

Some seeds need treatment to damage the seed coat, thereby ending dormancy and promoting germination. This happens in Nature when animals eat fruits containing seeds, which pass through the digestive tract. The acidic environment of the digestive tract etches the seed coat and promotes germination. A damaged seed coat allows moisture into the seed, which starts the germination process once other conditions are met. A plant propagator can simulate the *scarification* process by using one or more of the following methods.

- Soak seeds in boiling water or very strong black coffee
- Nick large seeds with a knife (*Pinus sabiniana*, for example)
- Line a jar with sandpaper or grit; add seeds and shake

In some cases, seeds will require scarification and stratification to promote germination. To figure out which methods might work, it helps to "think like Nature." For example, *Pinus sabiniana* produces large, nutritious seeds that squirrels relish. The squirrels may eat most of the seeds in each large cone, but some will be damaged (scarified) and overlooked because of the abundance of seed. These seeds, lying on the ground, will soon be covered and trod into the duff by other foragers and they will experience shorter days and falling temperatures—possibly even a light snow pack.

Propagation Equipment. Containers for seeds should be at least two inches deep. Sterilize recycled containers with a mild household bleach solution. Many native perennials, especially shrubs and trees, grow best in liners or tree-pots. *Overhead light* works best for germinating seeds. Fluorescent shop lights work, but a Gro-light set-up allows you to adjust the distance (two inches above the seed containers is optimal). When seeds have germinated, raise the lights to make sure tender young leaves do not get burned. *A propagation or heat mat* will heat the soil temperature to about 70 degrees, which will speed up germination and give you a head start on summer vegetables and flowers. *Keep the growing medium moist* for good germination and to keep new seedlings from drying out. Plastic lids designed to fit over the seed tray help maintain moisture. Undyed burlap or a sheet of newspaper can be laid directly on the soil surface for seeds that germinate in darkness. Check on seeds daily and remove any coverings at the first sign of green shoots. *Tip:* Dust the surface of newly seeded flats with cinnamon, which is a natural anti-fungal, to prevent molds and fungus from growing. Water seedlings with a very light mist sprayer or hand-held bottle sprayer. Always use room temperature water.

Soil Components and Mixes. Soil components are either organic (peat, coir, sphagnum, fir bark, compost, humus, vermicompost) or mineral (perlite, pumice, vermiculite, lava sand or rock, river sand). Use good quality soil with a high organic content as your basic ingredient, then "lighten it up" for nursery containers, or customize your soil mix for plants with special requirements.

- Peat moss or coir fiber adds moisture-retention qualities.
- Sphagnum moss may slow or stop certain plant diseases, including "damping-off."
- Perlite has no nutrient value but lightens the mix and helps ensure good drainage.
- Vermiculite has some available minerals, retains some water, and aids with drainage.
- Lava rock improves drainage. Use 5/16 or 3/8 sizes. Lava sand is a good choice in a mix for succulents.

- Coarse river sand promotes fast drainage. Never use playbox or beach sand.
- Vermicompost, worm-cast compost, is an excellent component in a soil mix. You can purchase or raise your own red wrigglers for their castings.

There are many ways to combine the above components. A seed-starting mix might combine equal parts of peat moss, fine perlite, vermiculite, and vermicompost. For two-inch pots: two parts of soil or compost and one part each of perlite and peat moss. For four-inch pots: three parts soil, one part each of peat moss and perlite and (unless seedlings are very delicate) one part lava rock. For one-gallon pots: three parts soil and one part each of peat moss, perlite and lava rock. For species that need a drier, very fast-draining mix, add one part coarse river sand.

Always work with a moist soil mix—and for best results with transplants, work in the shade and avoid unnecessary or prolonged exposure of sensitive roots to the air. Newly transplanted seedlings need to be kept in shade and babied for the first few days. Gradually expose the small plants to conditions normal for the plant species.

Cloning. Propagating by cuttings results in a clone of the parent plant. The ideal time to take cuttings of many species is when the plant is putting energy into fresh, new growth. A mature shrub can be "prepped" for cloning by pruning it to encourage new growth, then taking advantage of this new growth for tip or greenwood cuttings. Other plants are best propagated when dormant. When a mature plant is putting its energy into setting flowers or fruit, there will be less energy directed to cellular growth. For best results take cuttings in the morning, if possible, and immediately wrap them in moist paper towels and place them in a plastic bag. Keep them in a cool place (they will hold in a refrigerator wrapped like this for up to a week) until you have time to process the cuttings.

- *Leaf cuttings.* The cut leaf must generate both root and shoot, but some plants such as succulents and begonias can be propagated from leaf cuttings.
- *Herbaceous cuttings.* When taking cuttings of succulents, allow a couple of days for scar tissue to form over the cut before placing the cuttings in a moist rooting medium.
- *Tip cuttings.* Tip cuttings of new spring growth wilt easily and are prone to bruising and rot, but later in the season, while the growth is still young, you can see the base of the stem darkening and feel the stem firming. These tip cuttings will root more easily.
- *Semi-ripe cuttings.* Still later in the season, the stems are harder and buds can be seen developing at the nodes. Cuttings will be from this year's growth but the plant is not actively producing new growth at this time.
- *Hardwood cuttings.* These cuttings are taken when the plant is dormant.
- *Layering.* This process works well for vines and canes. Do not detach the "cutting" from the mother plant but place a node on the stem directly on the soil. When there is substantial new root growth, cut the clone from the mother plant.

- *Root cuttings*. Sections of root pieces are taken, which generally, but not always, produce clones. Some plants, known as "periclinal chimeras," produce a plant different from the parent. For example, variegated leaves in a number of plants are caused by a variety of plant disorders; tip cuttings from these plants inherit the malfunctioning cells and also display the variegation, but shoots and leaves formed from root cuttings are derived from cells that contain the plant's basic genetic information, so the shoots and leaves will produce solid green leaves.

Basic components of a rooting medium are perlite, vermiculite, peat moss, and coarse river sand. Which mix you choose depends on the species you plan to clone and the type of watering or misting system you have in place. Avoid rooting plants in water. Although some plants will grow roots in water, they often do not survive transplanting to soil. Avoid using a soil mix to root cuttings or planting a cutting in the garden, which exposes the cutting to potential pathogens. While some very hardy plants might grow anyway, results are more reliable in a soil-less mix. Experiment with different mediums. Some gardeners use only perlite, others will mix in sand or mix peat moss with either perlite or vermiculite. Sand can be used as a rooting medium but needs a misting system to keep cuttings constantly moist. *An all-purpose rooting mix:* use equal parts perlite, vermiculite, and peat moss. Remove most of the foliage and plan to keep the rooting medium and the cuttings consistently moist. Cuttings need a moist environment with light shade to promote the growth of new roots. Without a misting system, you may need to water several times a day.

Some plants are so easy to divide (asters, goldenrod, yarrow) that this is the best way to propagate them. When you dig up a mature, crowded clump for division, you have an opportunity to re-invigorate the plant by adding some compost and giving the plant more room to grow. Spring-blooming plants are best divided in fall; fall-blooming plants in winter or very early spring. For more information on how to propagate specific native plants, see Dara E. Emery's *Seed Propagation of Native California Plants*, published by the Santa Barbara Botanic Garden or Jeanine De Hart's *Propagation Secrets for California Native Plants* (self-published, jdhart@sbcglobal.net). *Making More Plants: The Science, Art, and Joy of Propagation* by Ken Druse (Clarkson Potter Publishers, 2000) and *Propagation Handbook: Basic Techniques for Gardeners* by Geoff Bryant (Stackpole Books, 1995) are good general references on how to propagate plants.

For the home propagator, there is much to be learned and little to lose. Don't be afraid to try a species using some of these basic guidelines. If in doubt, divide your seed or cuttings into different lots and use different methods, or timing, to learn which one yields the best results. There is nothing quite as satisfying, when admiring a mature tree or shrub or a beautiful drift of perennials in your garden, as knowing that you nurtured those plants from a mere seed or cutting. Plus, you will always have plants to share with your gardening friends!

APPENDIX B

Native Plant Communities

alifornia's major native plant communities include forest, woodland, grassland, chaparral, coastal scrub, desert scrub, alpine, and wetland communities. Within each community are dominant plants that characterize that plant community—evergreen shrubs of the chaparral community, for example, coast redwoods of the redwood forest community, bunchgrasses of the grassland communities. Plant communities may overlap, however, and some species from one plant community may be found in another. Some native plants, blue elderberry (*Sambucus mexicana*) and evening primrose (*Oenothera hookeri*), for example, thrive in both riparian and summer-dry areas. Knowing which plants grow together, with the same environmental conditions, makes choosing native plants for the garden much easier. For inspiration, take a walk in nearby open space or a preserve or botanical garden with a native plant section—a wildflower walk in spring, for example, with a county naturalist, your local chapter of the California Native Plant Society, or any of the many organizations that sponsor outings on protected lands. It is an easy and delightful way to learn the local flora and fauna. *Designing California Native Gardens* by Glenn Keator and Alrie Middlebrook is an excellent resource for locating native plant communities and for choosing native plant combinations within these plant communities for the garden. (See Appendix J, Books and Resources)

The four major California plant communities described below—chaparral, coastal scrub, mixed evergreen forest, and oak woodlands—may overlap and/or share some of the same native plants. Though not an inclusive summary of available plants for the garden, typical plants from each plant community are listed. Suggestions for riparian woodland gardens follow.

Chaparral

Dominated by evergreen shrubs, the chaparral plant community covers dry, rolling inland hills several miles from the coast. Chaparral plants are deep-rooted, drought tolerant and adapted to lean, rocky soils. Garden plants from this community need good drainage and full sun. The aromatic leaves of chaparral plants are designed to conserve moisture and are generally unappetizing to deer. Adapted to fire, chaparral plants regenerate quickly after a burn. Due to the volatile oils in the plant, it is best to locate them away from structures. Improve drainage by growing chaparral plants on mounds or berms.

Shrubs: Manzanita (*Arctostaphylos* spp.), California wild lilac (*Ceanothus* spp.), hollyleaf cherry (*Prunus ilicifolia*), coffeeberry (*Rhamnus* spp.), silk-tassel bush

(*Garrya elliptica*), Cleveland sage (*Salvia clevelandii*), Brandegee sage (*S. brandegeei*), purple sage (*S. leucophylla*), bush poppy (*Dendromecon rigida*)

Perennials, annuals, and grasses: California fuchsia (*Epilobium* spp.), foothill penstemon (*Penstemon heterophyllus*), matilija poppy (*Romneya coulteri*), narrowleaf milkweed (*Asclepias fascicularis*), buckwheat (*Eriogonum* spp.), bush monkeyflower (*Mimulus aurantiacus*), coyote mint (*Monardella* spp.), deergrass (*Muhenbergia rigens*), purple needlegrass (*Nassella pulchra*)

Coastal Scrub

Northern coastal scrub grows on the lower slopes of ocean-facing hills in the coastal summer-fog zone. Soils tend to be lean and rocky; winter rainfall, moderate to heavy. The dominant evergreen shrubs of this dense plant community are coyote bush and aromatic sages. Many bird species use coyote bush for cover, nesting, and foraging. This multifunctional fall-blooming evergreen shrub provides nectar for pollinators and seeds and insects for birds and other insect predators.

When setting seed, the flowers of St. Catherine's lace (*Erigonum giganteum*) fade to a lovely rust color. PHOTOGRAPH BY MIEKO WATKINS.

Shrubs: Coyote bush (*Baccharis pilularis*), California blackberry (*Rubus ursinus*), California wild lilac (*Ceanothus* spp.), creambush (*Holodiscus discolor*), osoberry (*Oemleria cerasiformis*), huckleberry (*Vaccinium ovatum*), wax myrtle (*Myrica californica*), California sagebrush (*Artemisia californica*), bush monkeyflower (*Mimulus aurantiacus*), various lupine (*Lupinus*) species, black sage (*Salvia mellifera*)

Perennials and annuals: Cow parsnip (*Heracleum lanatum*), seaside daisy (*Erigeron glaucus*), coast iris (*Iris douglasiana*), checkerbloom (*Sidalcea malviflora*), hedge nettle (*Stachys bullata*), California aster (*Aster chilensis*), tidy tips (*Layia platyglossa*), baby blue eyes (*Nemophila menziesii*), creamcups (*Platystemon californicus*), common meadowfoam (*Limnanthes douglasii*—seeps, moist areas)

The dominant scrub plants of the Southern California coastal area are California sagebrush, buckwheat, and cacti. While the predominantly gray-green foliage of southern coastal scrub may look less perky in the summer-dormant season, winter rains bring new growth in spring.

Shrubs: California sagebrush (*Artemisia californica*), buckwheat (*Eriogonum* spp.), lemonade berry (*Rhus integrifolia*), southern bush mallow (*Malacothamnus fasciculatus*), black sage (*Salvia mellifera*), purple sage (*S. leucophylla*), white sage (*S. apiana*), bladderpod (*Isomeris arborea*), island snapdragon (*Galvezia speciosa*), lupine (*Lupinus* spp.)

Perennials and grasses: Lilac verbena (*Verbena lilacina*), coast aster (*Lessingia filaginifolia*), California brittlebush (*Encelia californica*), showy milkweed (*Asclepias speciosa*), purple three-awn (*Aristida purpurea*), many species of cacti and succulents

Mixed Evergreen Forest

Forest habitats are diverse, multi-layered, peppered with streams and seeps. Evergreen trees dominate the forest, allowing sunlight to filter through the canopy to the shady understory of shrubs, ferns, lichens, perennials, and grasses. Decaying leaves and other organic matter make soils deep and fertile. Mixed evergreen forest communities, dominated by Douglas fir, are more prevalent in central and northern California. They may overlap with the redwood forest community where coastal redwoods reign and where moisture from coastal fog and a cooler summer climate prevail. Farther inland, forest communities may overlap with the drier oak woodland community.

Woodland plant combinations (coastal influence, moister soils): Coast redwood (*Sequoia sempervirens*), coast live oak (*Quercus agrifolia*), vine maple (*Acer circinatum*), California hazelnut (*Corylus cornuta*), Western rosebay (*Rhododendron macrophyllum*), California wax myrtle (*Myrica californica*), creambush (*Holodiscus discolor*), huckleberry (*Vaccinium ovatum*)

Ferns and perennials: Western sword fern (*Polystichum munitum*), five-finger fern (*Adiantum aleuticum*), lady fern (*Athyrium filix-femina*), wild ginger (*Asarum caudatum*), redwood sorrel (*Oxalis oregana*), Dutchman's pipe (*Aristolochia californica*)

Oak Woodlands

California's signature native plant community is oak woodlands. Before the widespread grazing of cattle and human development, oak savannah covered vast areas from the coast to interior valleys to rolling foothills. Unlike the closed canopy of forest plant communities, oak woodlands display a more open and rounded canopy. Shrubs, perennials, annual wildflowers, and grasses form the understory. Decomposing leaf litter from the oaks and their companion plants enriches the soil, making it more fertile than the lean soils of coastal scrub and chaparral communities. Evergreen oaks include coast live oak (*Quercus agrifolia*), interior live oak (*Q. wislizenii*), canyon live oak (*Q. chrysolepis*), island oak (*Q. tomentella*). Deciduous oaks include black oak (*Q. kelloggii*), blue oak (*Q. douglasii*), valley oak (*Q. lobata*), Oregon oak (*Q. garryana*), Engelmann oak (*Q. engelmannii*). (See Appendix C, Oaks in the Landscape, for oak-compatible plants.)

Riparian / Woodland Plant Communities

Plants grow in sun and shade conditions in streamside plant communities where there is year-round moisture and, generally, a dense understory of shrubs and ground plants. However, some plants from this community are drought

tolerant and can be found in other plant communities; blue elderberry, for example, is part of the oak woodland community and adapts to coastal and drier inland sites. The following plants are commonly used near ponds, along streams, and for creek restoration projects.

Trees and shrubs: Willow (*Salix* spp.), alder (*Alnus* spp.), red-twig dogwood (*Cornus sericea* and other *Cornus* spp.), blue elderberry (*Sambucus mexicana*), vine maple (*Acer circinatum*), Western spice bush (*Calycanthus occidentalis*), twinberry (*Lonicera involucrata*)

Perennials and grasses: California pipevine (*Aristolochia californica*), stream sedge (*Carex nudata*), brook orchid (*Epipactis gigantea*), scarlet monkeyflower (*Mimulus cardinalis*), creek monkeyflower (*M. guttatus*), yellow-eyed grass (*Sisyrinchium californicum*), rush (*Juncus* spp.)

The dark red stems of red-twig dogwood (*Cornus sericea*) look dramatic in winter when the foliage has disappeared.
PHOTOGRAPH BY MIEKO WATKINS.

APPENDIX C

Oaks in the Landscape

Oaks may be the most valuable plant for wildlife in California. Oak woodlands provide food and shelter for a myriad of wildlife species. Nutritious acorns feed insects, woodpeckers and jays, deer and many small mammals. In fact, all parts of the oak—from acorns and pollen to sap and leaves—are food sources for insects and mammals. Oaks attract many insects, which, in turn, feed many bird species, reptiles, and amphibians. Oaks offer shelter and nesting sites; oak cavities, in particular, are sought by woodpeckers, bluebirds, swallows, some owl species, and other cavity nesters. The oaks receive payback for their nurturing as squirrels, jays, and woodpeckers carry away their acorns to hide in secret places, often under the soil, where new oak seedlings can take root. Unfortunately many have been lost to human development and to human error in caring for them in the landscape. A native oak's natural conditions are winter rains and summer drought.

Keep your native oaks healthy by following these guidelines:

- Do not water under mature oaks. Watering during warm weather sets up conditions for pathogens and fungi to flourish. Although it may take ten years for a mature oak to die, frequent watering will eventually kill it. Water newly planted oaks only until established.

- Allow a thin layer of leaves to accumulate under trees, or mulch with tree chips three to six feet from the base out to the drip line. Roots should be visible near the trunk.

- Minimize pruning.

- Avoid cutting the roots, paving, or trenching within the root zone or compacting the soil with foot traffic, parked cars, or construction.

- When planting around or under oaks, use plants that do not need supplemental water during the dry months.

The following native plants, which thrive in dry shade to part shade, are suitable for planting under and around oaks and do not need supplemental water once established. Avoid drip irrigation and hand water new plants as necessary the first summer. Plants growing under deciduous oaks—black oaks, blue oaks, and valley oaks—receive more light in early spring than those growing under coast live oaks and other evergreen oaks.

Perimeter and Background Trees and Shrubs

Blue elderberry (*Sambucus mexicana*). Fast-growing deciduous large shrub with showy clusters of creamy flowers in spring, edible blue berries very attractive to birds, 10-30 feet tall.

California buckeye (*Aesculus californica*). A multi-branched deciduous tree that drops leaves early, silvery gray trunk, showy spikes of creamy, fragrant flowers in spring, very attractive to butterflies, native bees (but poisonous to honeybees), and hummers, 20-40 feet tall.

Coffeeberry (*Rhamnus californica*). Multifunctional, attractive shrub, tiny nectar flowers for pollinators in spring, berries for birds, host plant for several butterflies, 6-10 feet tall. 'Mound San Bruno' is a smaller variety.

Creambush (*Holodiscus discolor*). A deciduous shrub with creamy, fragrant clusters of flowers in spring, pretty apple-green foliage, butterfly host plant, 8 x 5 feet.

Hazelnut (*Corylus cornuta* var. *californica*). Fast-growing deciduous tree, produces edible nuts in late summer, to 15 feet.

Oregon grape (*Berberis/Mahonia aquifolium*). Evergreen shrub with glossy, spiny leaves, masses of yellow flowers in spring, berries for birds, 6 x 5 feet.

Pink-flowering currant (*Ribes sanguineum* var. *glutinosum*). An airy, semi-deciduous understory shrub with showy racemes of pink flowers in early spring, very attractive to hummingbirds, berries for birds, upright growth habit to 6 feet, especially beautiful when massed.

Snowberry (*Symphoricarpos albus*). Small, arching, and airy deciduous shrub with small pink flowers in spring, white round berries in fall, 3-5 feet tall.

Toyon (*Heteromeles arbutifolia*). Small evergreen tree or large shrub with dark green, glossy foliage, small white flowers in early summer, and bright red winter berries loved by Cedar Waxwings, Mockingbirds, and other bird species, 6-10 feet (taller in the wild).

Perennials, Grasses, and Other Groundcovers Three Feet or Under

Blue-eyed grass (*Sisyrinchium bellum*). Clumping perennial with bluish-green iris-like leaves and star-shaped blue flowers, very attractive in drifts, 8-10 inches high.

Bush monkeyflower (*M. aurantiacus* and hybrids). Shrubby perennial with large orange flowers and sticky leaves, cultivars of different colors, butterfly host plant and nectar plant for pollinators, to 3 feet high.

California buckwheat (*Eriogonum fasciculatum*). Mounding perennial with gray-green leaves and cream-colored flowers from summer to fall, butterfly host plant and nectar plant for pollinators, 2-3 feet tall.

California fescue (*Festuca californica*). Perennial, graceful cool-season bunchgrass, flowering stalks two feet or more above leaves, deer proof; cover, seeds, foraging, and nesting materials for birds, 2 x 2 feet.

Coral bells, alumroot (*Heuchera maxima, H. micrantha*). Mounding perennials with rounded scalloped leaves, flower stalks to 2 feet with tiny white to pink bell-shaped flowers from spring into summer; divide established plants in fall.

Douglas iris (*Iris douglasiana*). Clumping evergreen perennials in cream, yellow, blue, and lavender shades. *Iris douglasiana* 'Canyon Snow' is white with yellow markings. Pacific coast hybrids are bred from native iris species and include many beautiful color selections.

Manzanita (*Arctostaphylos* 'Emerald Carpet', *A. edmundsii* 'Carmel Sur', *A. hookeri* 'Monterey Carpet') and other low-growing manzanita species. Evergreen shrubs that provide cover for groundnesting birds, spring-blooming nectar flowers for hummingbirds, bees, and other pollinators.

Purple needlegrass (*Nassella pulchra*). Our state grass is found in oak woodlands, grasslands, and chaparral plant communities, clumps 2 feet tall and flower stalks up to 3 feet high.

Sages (*Salvia* spp.). Attractive to native bees, butterflies, and hummingbirds.
- Sonoma sage (*S. sonomensis*). Fast-growing, fragrant groundcover for banks and other areas, dark lavender flowers, to 6 feet wide.
- Hummingbird sage (*S. spathacea*). Large sticky leaves, fuchsia-colored flower spikes, spreads by rhizomes, to 3 feet high.

Western columbine (*Aquilegia formosa*). Woodland perennial with red-and-yellow flowers, attractive to hummers, 1-3 feet tall.

Western sword fern (*Polystichum munitum*). Upright evergreen fern with long leathery green fronds, year-round cover for birds and other creatures; remove older fronds to keep tidy.

Woodland strawberry (*Fragaria vesca*). A beautiful, spreading groundcover 6-8 inches tall, edible berries attractive to many bird species and small mammals.

Annual wildflowers: Elegant madia (*Madia elegans*), Chinese houses (*Collinsia heterophylla*), clarkia (*Clarkia* spp.), phacelia (*Phacelia* spp.), baby blue eyes and five-spot (*Nemophila* spp.).

Insects and Oaks

The following oak tree manifestations from insect damage, disease, or other causes may be visually unattractive but normally do not affect the health of the trees.

Oak moths. The native oak moth and oak trees have evolved together over a very long time. Defoliation caused by the moth caterpillars is cyclical—it can be minor in some years and more severe when there is a population boom. Though oaks may be defoliated, they have adapted to the moth and are rarely killed by oak moth damage. Spraying the tree with an insecticide is rarely necessary.

Acorn weevils and drippy nut disease. Damaged acorns, whether from weevils or a bacterial affliction called drippy nut disease (acorns ooze a sticky residue), do not indicate a more serious problem, nor do the oaks need treatment of any kind.

Galls. Growths, or galls, on the leaves and stems of oaks provide homes and nourishment for the larvae of many different species of tiny gall wasps. Enzymes from the larvae cause plant tissues to grow into structures of many sizes and shapes—from turbans and strawberries to stars and baseballs! Larvae may be parasitized or preyed on and adult gull wasps are food for birds and spiders; adults that survive look for a new host tree for the next generation. While leaves and twigs adjacent to the galls may be harmed, the tree itself is not adversely affected. Gall wasps do not sting and their galls are fascinating to observe. Blue oaks, which host the greatest number of gall wasp species, are the best choice for observing "gall art"!

Mistletoe. Common mistletoe (*Phoradendron flavescens*), which may hang in clumps from oak branches, is a mild parasite that uses some of the oak's nutrients but makes its own food through photosynthesis. Minor infestations are not normally a significant problem. Mistletoe does have wildlife value: it is the only caterpillar food plant for the Great Purple Hairstreak, a small butterfly with red-and-green markings and an orange abdomen. Deer eat the plant and birds feed on the berries.

Moss. The appearance of moss on trees, in the canopy, or on the trunk, is not a sign that the tree is unhealthy.

Carpenter worms/beetles. If you find swarms of carpenter worms or beetles on your tree, it is too late to do anything once the tree has been colonized. Spraying the tree with an insecticide will kill the insects but will not reverse the damage because the tree cannot build new wood.

Sudden Oak Death

Sudden oak death is a disease of oak trees caused by an invasive plant pathogen, *Phytophthora ramorum*. It is estimated to have killed more than one million oak and tanoak trees during the last decade. In addition, more than 100 other plant species are susceptible to the pathogen, but most suffer only minor damage limited to leaf spots or twig dieback. In California, it thrives in the coastal tanoak/redwood forests and oak woodlands within the fog belt. The oaks most affected by this disease are black oaks (*Quercus kelloggii*), live oaks (*Q. agrifolia*) and tanbark oaks (*Lithocarpus densiflorus*). Although sudden oak death is a forest disease, it can present many challenges for residential landscapes. Once sudden oak death infects oak trees, there is no known way to cure them. Therefore, most management practices are directed at preventing the spread of the disease to new plants or areas and protecting susceptible trees before they are infected. Diagnosis of infected trees and proper disposal of contaminated wood and other material are essential to limiting the spread of the disease. Management options include preventive treatment with phosphonate compounds and selective plant removal. More information can be found online at www.suddenoakdeath.org. (Adapted by Janice Alexander from the UC IPM Sudden Oak Death Pest Note, September 2010.)

For additional information about oaks, plant choices, and oak care, see the California Oak Foundation's website: www.californiaoaks.org.

APPENDIX D
Plants for Hedgerows

Coffeeberry (*Rhamnus californica*), an ideal evergreen shrub for hedgerows, provides cover, food, and nectar for birds and beneficial insects.
PHOTOGRAPH BY PAT HUNT.

Hedgerows are havens for wildlife, but they also serve as windbreaks, privacy screens, and erosion control. Consider several factors when choosing plants for a hedgerow—height and width desired, function in the landscape, and the local soils and climate. Tall trees, such as willows, cottonwoods, box elder, and bay, double as cover and foraging sites and windbreaks. Native evergreen shrubs provide food and shelter for birds and other wildlife and attract many species of beneficial insects. Plant your hedgerow on a berm, if possible, *at least* six inches high, to provide good drainage and to protect the root crowns from collecting water. Depending on desired outcome, shrubs may be spaced as close as four to six feet for a dense thicket. Fill in spaces with grasses and nectar flowers while waiting for the hedgerow to grow. Use a mulch of leaves and ground-up plant trimmings until the hedge is mature enough to cover the soil and create its own mulch. Weed and irrigate the first several years until the hedgerow is established. A mature native-plant hedgerow (two to three years) is self-sustaining, low-maintenance, and drought tolerant.

The following evergreen shrubs, mostly natives, are commonly used in various combinations for hedgerow plantings:

California lilac (*Ceanothus* spp.). Ceanothus blooms in the spring, attracts pollinators, and shelters many beneficial insects, including ladybird beetles, hoverflies, and lacewings; birds feed on the seeds and insects it attracts; also butterfly host plant. Grow in sun, drought tolerant. Good choices for hedgerows include *Ceanothus* 'Blue Jeans' (5-6 feet), *C.* 'Concha' and 'Sky Lark' (6 feet), *C.* 'Ray Hartman' (15-20 feet).

California wild rose (*Rosa californica*). Pink nectar flowers in summer and rose hips for birds in fall, grows quickly into a thorny thicket. Grow in sun or part shade, drought tolerant. A combination of wild rose, coyote bush, and/or California blackberry (*Rubus ursinus*) would offer cover for quail and other ground-nesters, good bird habitat, and an impenetrable barrier.

Coffeeberry (*Rhamnus californica*). Easy to cultivate, beautiful foliage, fast-growing to 6 feet, small nectar flowers in spring attract pollinators and beneficial insects, succulent berries for birds in the fall. Grow in sun or part shade, drought tolerant. 'Mound San Bruno' has a rounded compact shape (4 feet), *R.* 'Eve Case' (5 feet).

Coyote bush (*Baccharis pilularis*). Fall-blooming shrub attracts over 400 insects, highly valuable bird habitat plant for cover, nesting, and foraging. Grow in sun, drought tolerant. For hedgerows, use *B. pilularis consanguinea* (to 8 feet). For groundcover, use dwarf coyote bush, such as *B. pilularis* 'Pigeon Point' or *B. pilularis* 'Twin Peaks', which grow 3-4 feet tall. The female plant is the most useful; the flowers attract insects and the seeds feed many bird species.

Note: See hedgerow combination of California lilac, coffeeberry, and coyote bush on pages 36-37.

Hollyleaf cherry (*Prunus ilicifolia*). Shiny, sharp-edged foliage resembles holly, though the leaves are not as prickly; fragrant ivory racemes offer nectar in spring, small dark red fruits in the fall, butterfly host plant, 10-25 feet. Grow in sun, drought tolerant. Catalina cherry (*P. lyonii*), native to the Channel Islands, is similar but leaf edges are smooth. For part shade conditions, grow Western chokecherry (*P. virginiana demissa*), a fast-growing deciduous shrub especially suitable for coastal areas and a butterfly host plant for the Lorquin's Admiral.

Manzanita (*Arctostaphylos* spp.). Wine-red trunks, pink bell-shaped flowers are early nectar source for bees and hummingbirds, fruit for birds. Grow in sun or part shade, drought tolerant. Large shrubs for hedgerows include *Arctostaphylos densiflora* 'Howard McMinn', 'Harmony', and 'Sentinel'.

Pacific wax myrtle (*Myrica californica*). Glossy green and aromatic foliage, catkin flowers, and small purple-brown fruit for wildlife, 10-30 feet. Grow in sun or part shade, drought tolerant, especially suitable for urban gardens and coastal sites. Flickers and warblers are particularly fond of this shrub.

Toyon (*Heteromeles arbutifolia*). Also known as Christmas berry for its bright red winter berries that attract many bird species, 6-15 feet high. Grow in sun or part shade, drought tolerant.

Smaller Shrubs

Oregon grape (*Berberis/Mahonia aquifolium*). Dense bushy shape provides cover, spiny, glossy green foliage, bright yellow nectar flowers in spring, fruit for birds, to 5 feet. Grow in sun or part shade, drought tolerant.

Saltbush (*Atriplex lentiformis breweri*). Dense, spreading habit, gray foliage, fast-growing, 7 x 8 feet. Grow in full sun, drought tolerant; especially suitable for alkaline soils and coastal conditions. Beach saltbush (*A. leucophylla*), native to coastal areas, about 12 inches high with a spreading habit, full sun, sandy soil, butterfly host plant.

Non-native Evergreen Shrubs

Bush germander (*Teucrium fruticans*). Silvery-gray leaves, small blue flowers in spring, 4-6 feet with equal spread, drought tolerant. Grow in sun with good drainage.

Grevillea 'Canberra'. Fast-growing, hardy shrub from Australia, stiff, dark green foliage, rose-colored flowers bloom most of year, to 10 feet with equal spread, drought tolerant, unappetizing to deer. Heaviest bloom period is winter; a very attractive plant to hummingbirds. Many other sun-loving *Grevillea* species of various sizes are available.

Also: Fruit trees—persimmon, pomegranate, crabapple, and many others—are especially attractive to birds; nectar flowers for pollinators.

Grevillea 'Canberra' can grow as high as 10 feet. Peak bloom time is winter when hummingbirds are the hungriest.
PHOTOGRAPH BY PAT HUNT.

Understory Perennials and Grasses

California aster (*Aster chilensis* 'Point St. George'). Low-growing, mounding groundcover, lilac flowers, butterfly host plant. Grow in sun, drought tolerant.

California buckwheat (*Eriogonum fasciculatum*), St. Catherine's lace (*E. giganteum*), red buckwheat (*E. grande rubescens*), *E. latifolium* (near the coast), and other species are drought tolerant; various buckwheat species serve as butterfly host plants.

California poppy (*Eschscholzia californica*). Orange and yellow varieties, self-seeds readily, long bloom period. Plant in full sun, drought tolerant.

Coast aster (*Lessingia filaginifolia* 'Silver Carpet'). Low, dense groundcover with silvery foliage and pink-lavender flowers, summer-fall bloom. Grow in full sun, good drainage, moderate to occasional water.

Goldenrod (*Solidago* spp.). *S. rugosa*, a non-native species, forms a spreading groundcover, golden flowers in the fall. *S. californica*, a native species, has short spikes of yellow flowers; prefers part shade and little to no water.

Narrowleaf milkweed (*Asclepias fascicularis*). Easy-to-grow perennial, blooms with white nectar flowers in summer, butterfly host plant. Plant in sun, drought tolerant.

Pacific gumplant (*Grindelia stricta*). Bright yellow daisy-like flowers from summer through fall and a spreading, mounding habit, drought tolerant. Plant in full sun.

Pearly everlasting (*Anaphalis margaritacea*). Perennial with tiny ivory flowers, woolly gray-green foliage, spreads easily, butterfly host plant, to 3 feet high. Plant in full sun.

Yarrow (*Achillea millefolium*). Summer- and fall-blooming perennial, fern-like leaves, mounding groundcover, flower stalks 2 feet high, drought tolerant. Plant in full sun to part shade.

Grasses: Deergrass (*Muhlenbergia rigens*) and fescues (*Festuca californica*, *F. rubra*), Pacific reed grass (*Calamagrostis nutkaensis*).

Trees and Shrubs for Streamside Planting/Riparian Restoration

Dozens of bird species, including migratory species, depend on riparian habitat for nesting and foraging. PRBO Conservation Science (www.prbo.org) lists the following as key riparian plants: box elder, cottonwood, valley oak, arroyo willow, sandbar willow, California blackberry, poison oak, snowberry, blue elderberry, big-leaf maple, California bay, Oregon ash, white alder, dogwood, wild rose, mugwort, rushes, wild azalea, and California wild grape.

Blue elderberry (*Sambucus mexicana*). This drought-tolerant, deciduous large shrub is also found in riparian areas. Large clusters of creamy white flowers in spring attract many beneficial insects, and edible blue berries feed tanagers, grosbeaks, and many other bird species, grows 10-20 feet high, sun to part shade.

Dogwood (*Cornus* spp.). Red-twig dogwood (*C. sericea*) has beautiful wine-red stems, dramatic in winter when leaves are gone; grows into a dense thicket offering cover and berries for many bird species, shade tolerant.

Evening primrose (*Oenothera hookeri*). This multifunctional biennial, easy to grow from seed, is completely drought tolerant but also found in riparian areas; showy bright yellow nectar- and pollen-rich flowers from spring into fall, 5-6 feet high, especially attractive to bees, seeds feed birds for many months. Rosette appears first year, followed by tall flowering stalks the second year. Needs full sun but adaptable to dry or watered sites.

Evergreen huckleberry (*Vaccinium ovatum*). Slow-growing evergreen shrub with lots of wildlife value. Small bell-shaped nectar flowers attractive to insects and hummingbirds, black fruit for birds in late summer. Though often found in riparian areas, it is drought tolerant when established; 3-9 feet tall, deer resistant.

Willow (*Salix* spp.) Willows attract assassin bugs, ladybird beetles, and tachinid flies; their nectar flowers are an early source of nectar for bees.

Also: Stream sedge (*Carex nudata*), yellow-eyed grass (*Sisyrinchium californicum*), giant chain fern (*Woodwardia fimbriata*), lady fern (*Athyrium filix-femina*), rushes (*Juncus* spp.).

APPENDIX E

Seasonal Plants for Hummingbirds

There are many excellent nectar plants for hummingbirds. Local chapters of the Audubon Society and the California Native Plant Society are generally good resources for hummingbird plant lists especially suited to your region and microclimate. The following list contains drought-tolerant or low-water-use plants for sun or part shade, unless otherwise noted.

^ Blooms most of the year

WINTER-SPRING BLOOM PERIOD

Trees and Shrubs

Australian fuchsia (*Correa* spp.). Spreading evergreen shrubs from low-growing varieties to 8 feet high, bell-like flowers, flower color varies, full sun to full shade, good drainage, occasional to moderate water, unappetizing to deer.

^Bladderpod (*Isomeris arborea*). Fast-growing, strongly scented shrub from the coastal sage scrub community, abundant golden flowers, blue-green foliage and showy seedpods, 4-5 feet high, needs good drainage.

California buckeye (*Aesculus californica*). Deciduous, multi-trunked tree with showy cascades of creamy flowers in spring, beautiful palmate leaves and light gray bark, distinctive, round seedpods, 30 feet high. All parts of the plant are poisonous; nectar flowers are very attractive to hummers, butterflies, and native bees, but poisonous to honeybees.

^Chuparosa (*Justicia californica*). Small, frost-tender shrub with bright red tubular flower clusters, good for rock gardens.

Currants/Gooseberry (*Ribes* spp.). Deciduous shrubs that bloom from winter through spring.
- Pink-flowering currant (*R. sanguineum* var. *glutinosum*). Deciduous, airy shrub, maple-like leaves, racemes of pink flowers in spring, 6-12 feet tall.
- Fuchsia-flowering gooseberry (*R. speciosum*). Found in coastal scrub and chaparral plant communities; drooping, bright red tubular flowers in late winter/spring, spiny branches, 4-8 feet tall.
- Chaparral currant (*R. malvaceum*). Fast-growing, deciduous shrub with pale pink blossoms in winter, full sun, to 8 feet tall.

^Flowering maple (*Abutilon* spp.). Evergreen shrubs with showy bell-shaped flowers, moderate water (less in part shade), 8-10 feet high.

^*Grevillea* spp. Hardy, drought-tolerant evergreen shrubs and trees from Australia, bright green, needle-like foliage, clusters of slender flowers very attractive to hummingbirds and other pollinators. *G.* 'Canberra' grows to 8 x 10 feet, rose-colored flowers most of year with heaviest bloom in winter, excellent choice for hedge, no summer water once established.

^Island bush snapdragon (*Galvezia speciosa*). Climbing, evergreen shrub with bright red flowers and sprawling habit, 3-4 feet, needs well-drained soil.

Lupine (*Lupinus* spp.). Many species of shrubs (and annuals and perennials) with "sweet-pea" clusters of flowers, mostly shades of blue.

Manzanita (*Arctostaphylos* spp.). Many species from creeping groundcover to large shrubs, smooth wine-red bark and small white to pink bell-shaped flowers, good source of late winter nectar for Anna's hummingbirds, berries for birds, good drainage, no supplemental water once established.

Pitcher sages (*Lepechinia fragrans, L. calycina*). Large, woody, sage-related shrubs from chaparral plant communities, white or lavender tubular flowers. *L. fragrans* is more aromatic, can take dry shade under oaks.

Sages (*Salvia* spp.)
- Black sage (*S. mellifera*). Chaparral evergreen shrub with dark green foliage and white flowers in spring, low-growing to upright varieties.
- Brandegee sage (*S. brandegeei*). Easy-to-grow vigorous evergreen shrub similar to black sage, pale lavender flowers, 3-5 feet tall.
- Purple sage (*S. leucophylla*). Evergreen shrub with pink to purple spikes, apple-green foliage turns silver-gray in summer, mounding varieties good choice for spilling over banks or on slopes.

Willow (*Salix* spp.). Many native and non-native species of deciduous trees/shrubs, tiny flowers early nectar source for hummers and bees, seeds for birds, good choice for streamside plantings and ponds, but adaptable to less water in garden settings.

Woolly blue curls (*Trichostema lanatum*). Evergreen shrub with fuzzy purple-blue flowers, 3-5 feet tall, best for hot, dry, sunny sites with good drainage.

Drought-tolerant pitcher sage (*Lepechinia* spp.) is highly attractive to hummingbirds. Pictured here is *Lepechinia calycina*. PHOTOGRAPH BY MIEKO WATKINS.

Perennials, Annuals, and Vines

California bee plant (*Scrophularia californica*). Tall perennial with tiny red flowers at top of long stems, sun to light shade, 3-6 feet tall.

Cape fuchsia (*Phygelius* spp.). Shrubby perennials with penstemon-like flowers in shades of peach, red, and yellow, native to South Africa, 3-4 feet tall.

Coral bells (*Heuchera maxima*, *H. micrantha*). Evergreen perennials, dense clumps of heart-shaped leaves, tiny white bell-shaped flowers, good choice for under oaks or woodland gardens, many hybrid species also available.

Honeysuckles (*Lonicera* spp.).
- Twinberry (*L. involucrata*). Deciduous shrub, tubular yellow-orange flowers followed by black berries, 5-8 feet tall.
- Trumpet honeysuckle (*L. sempervirens*). Climbing vine, large orange tubular flowers, 10-20 feet, moderate water.

Hummingbird mint (*Monardella macrantha*). Low-growing, trailing perennial, large red tubular flowers, needs good drainage.

Impatiens (*Impatiens balfourii*, *I. glandulifera*). Easy to grow annuals for shady locations, *I. balfourii*, 18 inches, pink/white flowers; *I. glandulifera*, much taller to 5 feet, white to lavender flowers, light shade best, both reseed easily.

Monkeyflowers (*Mimulus* spp.). Many hybrids available.
- Red monkeyflower (*M. puniceus*). Native to southern California, velvety red flowers, 3-4 feet high, full sun.
- Scarlet monkeyflower (*M. cardinalis*). Bright-orange tubular flowers, for bogs and moist sites, 1-2 feet high, full sun.
- Sticky monkeyflower (*M. aurantiacus* and hybrids). Shrubby perennial from chaparral plant community, yellow-orange flowers, to 3 feet high. Hybrids come in variety of colors.

SUMMER-FALL BLOOM PERIOD

Trees and Shrubs

Bottlebrush (*Callistemon* spp.). Fast-growing evergreen shrubs or trees from Australia with soft, brushlike, red flower clusters attractive to hummingbirds, full sun/part shade, low water once established.

Butterfly bush (*Buddleia* spp.). Large deciduous and evergreen shrubs, foliage from green to gray, spiky clusters of fragrant, nectar-rich flowers in magenta, lavender, white, purple, need good drainage.

Desert willow (*Chilopsis linearis*). Deciduous tree found at lower elevations and often in desert washes, lovely flowers in shades of rose and lavender, to 20 feet, full sun.

Sages (*Salvia* spp.). Many native and non-native species.
- Autumn sage (*S. greggii*). Many varieties of bushy evergreen or deciduous shrubs, flower color varies, 1-3 feet.
- Cleveland sage (*S. clevelandii*). Evergreen chaparral shrub, fragrant dark-blue flowers, 3-5 feet tall, full sun.
- Mexican bush sage (*S. leucantha*). Hardy evergreen shrub, long lavender spikes, gray-green foliage, 3-4 feet tall.
- *S.* 'Phyllis's Fancy'. Hardy evergreen shrub, lavender-tinged white flowers, 4-5 feet tall, blooms summer into winter.

Strawberry tree (*Arbutus unedo*). Evergreen tree or shrub, reddish-bark with white clusters of urn-shaped flowers and yellow-and-red fruit in late summer, to 35 feet; 'Compacta' to 10 feet high.

Perennials, Annuals, and Vines

Fragrant Cleveland sage (*Salvia clevelandii*) attracts hummingbirds, bees, and other pollinators.
PHOTOGRAPH BY MIEKO WATKINS.

Agastache (*Agastache* spp.). Long-blooming perennial, flower spikes of varied colors, 2-3 feet tall, moderate water.

Bee balm (*Monarda didyma*). Bushy perennial, fragrant foliage, tubular flowers in shades of pink, red, and purple, spreads easily, a hummingbird favorite, full sun, regular water.

Blood-red trumpet vine (*Distictis buccinatoria*). Tender, fast-growing vine, abundant orange-red tubular flowers, good choice for coastal gardens, full sun to light shade, good drainage, occasional water, native to Mexico.

California fuchsia (*Epilobium* spp., also known as *Zauschneria*). Gray-green foliage, scarlet tubular flowers, many varieties, 1-3 feet tall, full sun.

Cardinal flower (*Lobelia cardinalis*). Bright red flowers, good bog plant, sun, native to mountains of southern California.

Penstemon spp. Many native and non-native species, easy to grow, tubular flowers in many colors, generally needs good drainage. (See species listed under Snapdragon Family in Appendix G.)

Red-hot poker, torch lily (*Kniphofia uvaria*, *K.* hybrids). Clumping grass-like foliage, showy torch-like nectar-rich flowers in red, orange, yellow that hummers—and orioles—love. Likes moist conditions, but drought tolerant, deer resistant.

Sages (*Salvia* spp.).
- Anise-scented sage (*S. guaranitica*). Lush, dark foliage with blue-purple spikes, likes part shade, some supplemental water, upright to 5 feet.

Sages (*Salvia* spp.) are very attractive to hummingbirds. Pictured here is *Salvia leucantha.*

PHOTOGRAPH BY ROBERT WATKINS.

- Bog sage (*S. uliginosa*). Vigorous, airy perennial with light blue flowers for bogs and other moist areas, to 6 feet tall, 3-4 feet wide.
  - Hummingbird sage (*S. spathacea*). Clumping perennial, large, coarse leaves, magenta flower spikes above the foliage, spreads by rhizomes, works well as mounding groundcover, prefers light shade, drought tolerant but likes garden water; deer dislike the sticky leaves.
  - Pineapple sage (*S. elegans*). Bushy, tender perennial with bright red flowers, citrus-scented foliage, 3-4 feet.
  - Scarlet sage (*S. coccinea*). Bushy annual from Mexico with long bloom period, short red spikes and dark green foliage; 'Lady in Red' favorite choice for hummingbirds, 2 x 2 feet.
  - *S.* 'Indigo Spires', *S.* 'Waverly'. Shrubby perennials with long violet spikes and long bloom periods, sun/part shade, to 6 feet tall.

Trumpet creeper (*Campsis radicans*). Vigorous, semi-deciduous vine to 40 feet, large orange tubular flowers, full sun/part shade, low water once established.

APPENDIX F

Common California Butterflies and Host Plants

The following list of California butterflies describes some of the species most commonly seen in gardens. Urban gardens may attract different species from gardens near open space, forests, or parklands, and populations of common butterflies can vary substantially from one region to another, and within the same county. Butterfly host plant lists vary, too. Check with your chapter of the California Native Plant Society, local garden clubs, or native plant nurseries for butterfly species usually seen in your area, and the caterpillar food plants that are most successful. The North American Butterfly Association's web site (www.naba.org) offers regional information on butterflies, and nectar and host plants. One naturalist I know recommends planting a butterfly bush (*Buddleia* spp.), then observe which butterflies come to the garden, learn the species and plant the caterpillar host plants. If host plants are small (perennials, vines, small shrubs), always grow at least three and group them together near nectar plants and, if possible, in different areas of the garden.

The Mourning Cloak butterfly uses willows and poplars as caterpillar food plants.
PHOTOGRAPH BY BOB STEWART.

Note: Butterfly size is the approximate measurement from wingtip to wingtip.

Anise Swallowtail. Large yellow-and-black butterfly with yellow rectangles on a black background, 3 1/2 inches. Caterpillar is green with black stripes and yellow-and-orange spots.

Carrot family (Apiaceae): Parsley, dill, bulbing fennel, bronze fennel (*Foeniculum* 'Purpurascens', *F*. 'Smokey'), lovage (*Levisticum officinale*), and angelica (*Angelica archangelica*). Native host plants include yampah (*Perideridia kelloggii* and other species), *Angelica tomentosa* and *A. hendersonii*, cow parsnip (*Heracleum lanatum*), *Lomatium californicum*.

Note: Common fennel (*Foeniculum vulgare*), the Anise Swallowtail's favored host plant, is invasive and not recommended for gardens. However, if you wish to grow it, be sure to cut it back before it goes to seed.

Pale Swallowtail. Large cream-and-black butterfly, similar to the Western Tiger Swallowtail, 3 3/8 - 3 3/4 inches, less likely in urban gardens. Caterpillar is green with large yellow eyespots.

California coffeeberry (*Rhamnus californica*), creambush (*Holodiscus discolor*), hollyleaf cherry (*Prunus ilicifolia*).

Western Tiger Swallowtail. Large yellow butterfly with four vertical black stripes, 3 1/2 - 4 3/8 inches. Caterpillar is green with large yellow eyespots.

Willows, alders, sycamores, cottonwoods.

American Lady. Medium-sized orange-and-black butterfly with white rectangle on edge of upper front wing, black upper hind wing spots are merged, 1 3/4 - 2 1/8 inches. Caterpillar has spines, black patches, and white spots.

Pearly everlasting (*Anaphalis margaritacea*) and cudweeds (*Gnaphalium californicum, G. palustre, G. purpureum,* and other native species; also *G. gluteo-album* [non-native]). *Gnaphalium californicum* is the most well behaved of the cudweeds.

Painted Lady. Medium-sized orange-and-black migrating butterfly found in more areas of the world than any other butterfly species, 2 - 2 3/4 inches. Caterpillar is mostly black with yellow stripes.

Mostly thistles: Cobweb thistle (*Cirsium occidentale*) and some non-native thistles. Also: Aster family (Asteraceae): pearly everlasting (*Anaphalis margaritacea*). Mallow family (Malvaceae): desert mallow (*Sphaeralcea ambigua*), chaparral mallow (*Malacothamnus fasciculatus*), Palmer's bush mallow (*Malacothamnus palmeri*), island mallow (*Lavatera/Malva assurgentiflora*). Weedy plants, such as cheeseweed (*Malva nicaensis, Malva parviflora*) and English plantain (*Plantago lanceolata*), are widely used as host plants.

West Coast Lady. Medium-sized orange-and-black butterfly similar to Painted Lady but with orange rectangle on leading edge of upper front wing, 1 3/4 - 2 inches. Caterpillar has yellow-and-black stripes.

Mallow family (Malvaceae): Checkerbloom (*Sidalcea malviflora*), island mallow (*Lavatera/Malva assurgentiflora*), desert mallow (*Sphaeralcea ambigua*), bush mallow (*Malacothamnus fasciculatus*), cheeseweed (*Malva nicaensis*), and other mallows; lupine (*Lupinus* spp.).

Note: Don Mahoney at the San Francisco Botanical Garden recommends trailing mallow (*Modiolastrum lateritum*) to attract West Coast Ladies. This easy-to-grow mallow from South America is hardy to 20 degrees and drought tolerant with salmon-pink flowers. Works well for banks or as a 1-foot-high ground cover.

Common Checkered Skipper. Small white-and-gray patterned butterfly, 1 - 1 1/8 inches. Caterpillar is white/brown with dark dots and streaks.

Mallow family (Malvaceae): Checkerbloom (*Sidalcea malviflora*), hollyhock (*Alacea rosea*), flowering maple (*Abutilon* spp.), desert mallow (*Sphaeralcea* spp.), and non-native weedy mallows, such as cheeseweed.

Common Buckeye. Medium-sized brown-and-orange butterfly with large eyespots, 1 3/8 - 2 1/2 inches. Caterpillar is black with spines and orange head.

Populations vary regionally, and from year to year.

Snapdragon family (Scrophulariaceae): creek monkeyflower (*Mimulus guttatus*), twinspur (*Diascia* spp.), purple owl's clover (*Castilleja exserta*), snapdragon (*Antirrhinum majus*), speedwell (*Veronica* spp.), toadflax (*Linaria* spp.), heart-leaved penstemon (*Keckiella cordifolia*), yellow bush penstemon (*K. antirrhinoides*). Plantain family (Plantaginaceae): plantain (*Plantago erecta, P. lanceolata*). Also: *Penstemon* spp., lippia or mat grass (*Phyla nodiflora*), and mare's tail (*Hippuris vulgaris*).

Variable Checkerspot. Medium-sized black butterfly with many yellow-and-red spots, 1 1/2 - 2 1/8 inches. Caterpillar is similar to the Common Buckeye butterfly, black with spines but head is black.

Snapdragon family (Scrophulariaceae). Bush monkeyflower (*Mimulus aurantiacus, M. longiflorus*), California bee plant (*Scrophularia californica*).

Mourning Cloak. Large dark brown butterfly with pale yellow border, may live up to 10 months by hibernating during the winter, 2 1/4 - 2 1/2 inches. Caterpillar is purplish-black with long spines and white speckles and a row of orange spots along sides.

Willows (*Salix* spp.) and *Populus* spp.—poplars, alders, cottonwoods; occasionally elm and birch.

Lorquin's Admiral. Large black-and-white butterfly with orange-tipped wings, more common in riparian areas, 2 1/8 - 2 7/8 inches. Caterpillar is splotchy with gray-and-white markings, resembles bird droppings.

Willows (*Salix* spp.), creambush (*Holodiscus discolor*), Western chokecherry (*Prunus virginiana* var. *demissa*).

Red Admiral. Medium-sized black butterfly with reddish-orange band, 2 inches. Caterpillar is white with short spines; binds leaves together with silken threads for shelter.

Nettle family (Urticaceae): Nettle (*Urtica holosericea*), baby tears (*Soleirolia soleirolii*), pellitory (*Parietaria judaica*). Also: hop vine (*Humulus* spp.).

California Sister. Large dark butterfly with white markings and orange spots at tip of wings, 2 3/8 - 3 1/2 inches. Caterpillar is dark green.

Oaks (*Quercus* spp.): Coast live oak (*Q. agrifolia*), canyon live oak (*Q. chrysolepis*), black oak (*Q. kelloggii*), and others.

Mournful Duskywing. Small dark butterfly with a white border on hind wings, 1 1/8 - 1 1/4 inches. Caterpillar is grayish-green with yellow stripe and white dots.

Coast live oak (*Quercus agrifolia*), blue oak (*Q. douglasii*), valley oak (*Q. lobata*).

Monarch. Large orange migrating butterfly, 3-4 inches. Last generation to migrate may live up to 8 months. Caterpillar has narrow stripes of black, yellow, and white.

Milkweed (*Asclepias* spp.).

Cabbage White. Medium-sized white butterfly, introduced from Europe, very common in gardens, 1 5/8 - 2 1/4 inches. Caterpillar is bright green.

Mustard family (Brassicaceae): cabbage family plants, wild mustard, and radish; nasturtium (*Tropaeolum majus*). *Arabis glabra* is a native butterfly host plant for nine species of whites and Sara Orangetip.

Orange Sulfur. Medium-sized yellow butterfly with a narrow black border on upper wings, 1 3/4 - 2 3/8 inches. Caterpillar is green with pale stripes along sides.

Pea family (Fabaceae): Lupines (*Lupinus* spp.), deerweed (*Lotus scoparius*), and other lotus species, clovers and vetches, alfalfa. *Lotus purshianus* serves eight species as a host plant, including Orange Sulfur, Common Hairstreak, and Acmon Blue butterflies.

Acmon Blue. Small, silvery-blue butterfly, 1/4 - 1 inch. When perching this butterfly moves its hind wings to flash orange "eye spots," a protective mechanism to encourage predators to bite its wing rather than its head. Caterpillar is yellow and hairy with green stripe.

Pea (Fabaceae) and buckwheat (Polygonaceae) families: Deerweed (*Lotus scoparius*) and other *Lotus* spp. Buckwheats (*Eriogonum latifolium, E. nudum, E. parvifolium, E. cinereum* [southern CA]). *Eriogonum nudum* is also a nectar and butterfly host plant for Mormon Metalmark, Bramble Hairstreak, Gorgon Copper, Dotted Blue, Square-spotted Blue, and others.

Silvery Blue. Small gray-blue butterfly, row of black dots on underwing, 1 - 1 1/4 inches. Caterpillar is bright green.

Pea family (Fabaceae): Deerweed (*Lotus scoparius*), lupines (*Lupinus* spp.), vetches (*Vicia* spp.).

Spring Azure. Small blue butterfly, 1 - 1 1/8 inches. Caterpillar is green, sometimes pink in color.

Chamise (*Adenostoma fasciculatum*), creambush (*Holodiscus discolor*), California lilac (*Ceanothus* spp.), California buckeye (*Aesculus californica*), redtwig dogwood (*Cornus sericea*).

Gray Hairstreak. Small gray butterfly with orange band and two large orange spots, 3/4 - 1 1/8 inches. Caterpillar is light brown/ rust colored.

Coffeeberry (*Rhamnus californica*), alfalfa, clovers, *Hibiscus* spp. (southern CA), and weedy non-native mallows such as cheeseweed.

Grass Skippers. Tiny butterflies in various patterns of gold, brown, and orange tones that hold their front wings mostly closed and hind wings out at a 45-degree angle when perching, 7/8 - 1 1/4 inches. The Fiery Skipper is very common in gardens with lawns.

Sedge (*Carex* spp.), California bunchgrasses, and other grass species.

Host plants for the Umber Skipper include hairgrass (*Deschampsia caespitosa*), San Diego sedge (*Carex spissa*), California brome (*Bromus carinatus*).

Host plants for the Woodland Skipper include rye grass (*Elymus* spp., especially *E. glaucus*). Both skippers are commonly seen in gardens.

Butterflies That May Be Common to Gardens in Specific Regions

Gulf Fritillary. Large orange-brown butterfly with silvery-white spots on underwings, found in coastal San Francisco and southward, 2 - 3 inches. Caterpillar is dark gray with spines and orange stripes.

Passion vine (*Passiflora* spp.): Blue-crown passionflower (*P. caerulea*) is much more caterpillar friendly than *P. alatocaerulea*.

Pipevine Swallowtail. Large, orange-spotted, iridescent bluish-black butterfly found in riparian areas of northern and central California, 3 - 3 1/2 inches. Caterpillar is red and black.

California pipevine (*Aristolochia californica*). Grow at least two, preferably three, vines. Slow to start while sinking deep roots, but generally takes off in second or third year. Caterpillars use only this species of pipevine and are not adapted to pipevines from other areas. *Note: A. elegans* is fatal to most larvae.

Marine Blue. Small bluish-brown butterfly with white and gray stripes on underwing, 1 inch, common in southern California. Caterpillar color varies from shades of green to brown.

Pea family (Fabaceae): Deerweed (*Lotus scoparius*), wisteria (*Wisteria* spp.), sweet pea (*Lathyrus* spp.), and other legumes.

Cloudless Sulphur. Large, bright yellow migrating butterfly, 2 inches, mostly found in southern California. Caterpillar is bright yellowish-green with yellow stripe.

Sennas (*Cassia* spp.).

California Dogface, state butterfly. Though this large yellow butterfly (2 - 2 1/2 inches) is our state butterfly, it is not commonly found in gardens. Its populations are found in scattered areas throughout California where the host plant is present. Caterpillar is green.

False Indigo (*Amorpha californica*, *A. fruticosa*); also host plant for Gray Hairstreak and other less common garden butterflies.

APPENDIX G

Top Nectar and Pollen Plant Families

The following plant families—aster, mint, carrot, pea, buckwheat, snapdragon, mallow, and verbena—are good sources of shrubs, perennials, and annuals for the wildlife garden. Especially rich in nectar and/or pollen, many also offer seed or fruit for birds or serve as host plants for butterflies. Unless otherwise noted, the following plant species are low-water-use plants. Various seed catalogs, especially those specializing in heirloom varieties of flowers and vegetables, are good sources for old-fashioned annuals and perennials that are not over-hybridized. Single-flowered versions of the composites, in particular, offer more nectar and pollen.

Aster/Sunflower Family (Asteraceae). The composites, members of the huge aster/sunflower family, are butterfly beacons with good perching platforms. Because their long-blooming, open-faced flowers are such excellent sources of both nectar and pollen, they serve as energy-efficient feeding stations for butterflies, bees, and other pollinators. Composites are mainstays of the summer nectar garden and a fall and winter seed source for finches, juncos, and other seed-eating bird species. They also provide chaff for nesting materials. Shrubs in the sunflower family provide cover and shelter and an insect food source for birds and other insect predators. The following list highlights both familiar composites and others that are less well known but highly recommended.

Aster (*Aster* spp.). Many aster species are widely available for summer through fall bloom.
- California aster (*Aster chilensis*). Perennial aster with lavender or white flowers in late summer, drought tolerant, butterfly host plant for the Field Crescent. *A. chilensis* 'Pt. St. George' has a mounding, spreading habit, good ground cover for sun/part shade for under trees or hedgerows.
- Coast aster, woolly aster (*Lessingia filaginifolia*). Perennial native of coastal areas, blooms in fall through December with lavender flowers, full sun, no summer water, forms ground cover, especially attractive to butterflies. 'Silver Carpet' is a popular variety.
- Michaelmas daisy/New England aster (*Aster nova-angliae*). A North American native perennial that blooms in October with masses of lavender flowers on tall stems, up to 6 feet tall. Plant a stand in the sun at the back of a fence or in the "wild" part of the garden where they will have room to grow; a bee and butterfly favorite.

Blanketflower (*Gaillardia* spp.). Perennial native to the plains states, hardy, long bloom period from early spring until late fall, sun, drought tolerant, maroon to red-and-yellow flowers. *G. aristata* is the wild form still found in some wildflower mixes; *G.* x *grandiflora* and hybrids. Avoid dwarf forms and varieties with large, showy flowers.

California brittlebush (*Encelia californica*). Native to coastal bluffs of southern California, this herbaceous shrub blooms frequently with showy, golden disks with chocolate centers, 2-4 feet tall, full sun, drought tolerant, good for banks for erosion control.

Coast goldenbush (*Isocoma menziesii* var. *menziesii*). Golden nectar flowers from spring until winter, hardy, drought-tolerant subshrub ideal for sunny sites or meadow gardens.

Cobweb thistle (*Cirsium occidentale*). A biennial native to coastal areas, this lovely thistle has silver foliage that resembles "webbing" and a beautiful flower; butterfly host plant for the Painted Lady and Mylitta Crescent. Plant in well-drained soil in full sun.

Coreopsis (*Coreopsis* spp.). Many summer-blooming annual and perennial varieties in shades of yellow, orange, maroon, and red.
- Plains coreopsis (*C. tinctoria*). Hardy annual native to the plains regions but quite adaptable to California's climate, profuse yellow nectar flowers with maroon centers, abundant seed for finches and other bird species in the fall.
- Sea dahlia (*C. maritima*). Native to southern coastal areas, this perennial has large golden daisy-like flowers.

Cosmos (*Cosmos bipinnatus, C. sulphureus*). Large flowers in pink, white, and purple bloom from summer through fall, birds love the seeds. *C. sulphureus* has yellow-orange flowers especially attractive to pollinators. Avoid frilly, showy varieties.

Coyote mint (*Monardella villosa*). Summer-to-fall-blooming nectar plant with lavender flowers for bees and butterflies, effective in drifts, full sun, occasional summer water. Scarlet coyote mint (*M. macrantha*). Short-lived, low-growing, trailing plant with large red tubular flowers, suitable for containers and rock gardens, needs good drainage and full sun.

Golden yarrow (*Eriophyllum confertiflorum*). Perennial with abundant golden flower clusters, 1-2 feet high, drought tolerant.

Goldenrod (*Solidago* spp.). Native and non-native perennial species. *Solidago rugosa* works well in flowerbeds or as a ground cover for fall bloom; *S. californica* spreads by rhizomes, better for wild or meadow gardens.

Gumplant (*Grindelia stricta*). Mounding, spreading groundcover especially suited for coastal sites, yellow, daisy-like flowers in summer contrast with ample green foliage, sun, drought tolerant or occasional summer water, adaptable to many kinds of soil.

Joe Pye weed (*Eupatorium purpureum*). Small pink flowers bloom from July through September in large clusters on sturdy green stems up to 7 feet in height. Grows best in moist soil in full to part sun, excellent butterfly nectar plant. For best germination rate, seeds should be cold-stratified for 2-4 weeks prior to planting. Needs staking.

Mexican sunflower (*Tithonia rotundifolia*). Annual with vigorous growth in sun and heat, vivid orange single flowers measure 3 inches across, blooms summer/fall, 4-6 feet high, very attractive to butterflies, seeds for finches, grosbeaks, and others.

Pearly everlasting (*Anaphalis margaritacea*). Butterfly host plant for the American Lady and other butterfly species, this perennial has gray-green foliage and tiny white flowers, about 2 feet high.

Purple coneflower (*Echinacea purpurea*). Summer-blooming perennial, large, deep pink flowers with bronze, dome-shaped centers on long stems, 2-3 feet high, tolerates moist soil, highly attractive to butterflies. Select a sunny location and plant seed in early spring. For best results, mix seed with a cup of sand for better distribution of seed over the planting area. Keep moist until plants begin to grow. Water only when necessary.

Seaside daisy (*Erigeron glaucus*). Ideal composite for coastal bluffs/sites, clumping, blue-green foliage and pink daisy flowers on short stems.

Sunflower (*Helianthus annuus*). Many varieties available, all descended from the wild sunflower native to the U.S. Avoid sunflowers classified as *H. x hybridus*, which do not have pollen. The perennial *H. maximilianii* forms a clump to 10 feet tall with light yellow 3-inch flowers.

Yarrow (*Achillea millefolium*). This native yarrow has white to pink flowers and green, fern-like leaves, blooms summer into fall, highly attractive to butterflies and other insects, good groundcover option. Many non-native yarrow hybrids available but native yarrow offers the most wildlife value.

Wildflowers: Tidy tips (*Layia platyglossa*), woolly sunflower (*Eriophyllum lanatum*), goldfields (*Lasthenia californica*), tarweeds (*Madia elegans, Hemizonia* spp.), and others.

Zinnia (*Zinnia* spp.). Annual flowers for fall bloom and a butterfly favorite; avoid pompom and dwarf varieties in favor of old-fashioned single-flowered varieties.

Mint Family (Lamiaceae). This large family of richly scented plants includes many sun-loving and drought-tolerant plants as well as culinary mints and riparian species that prefer more moisture. Mint family members are found in many native plant communities—desert, coastal scrub, chaparral, and forest.

Native yarrow (*Achillea millefolium*) blooms with white or pink flowers that are attractive to butterflies and other insects. PHOTOGRAPH BY MIEKO WATKINS.

Members of the mint family are good nectar sources for hummingbirds, bees, and other pollinators and they offer seeds and cover for birds.

Low-water/drought-tolerant species

Calamint (*Calamintha nepeta*). Bushy, compact Mediterranean perennial with masses of tiny nectar-rich white to pale lavender flowers in late summer loved by honeybees, full sun, well-drained soil, occasional water.

Catmint (*Nepeta* spp.). Hard working, Mediterranean shrubby perennial that blooms early and finishes late fall, scented foliage and blue flowers attractive to honeybees. Cut back old flower stems for new growth underneath.

Desert lavender (*Hyptis emoryi*). Gray, aromatic shrub with lavender flowers, sun, drought tolerant, sandy soil, good choice for southern California gardens.

Hedge nettle (*Stachys bullata*). Perennial herb, a favorite of butterflies, good as groundcover for full sun or part shade, woodland gardens or wild gardens, spikes of pink flowers, 6-8 inches high, occasional water for better flowering. *Note:* it can be invasive.

Hyssop (*Hyssopus officinalis*). Aromatic perennial with dark green foliage and dark blue flower spikes in summer, full sun, light shade, low water.

Lemon balm (*Melissa officinalis*). Though this lemon-scented bushy perennial from the Mediterranean region spreads rapidly, its tiny white flowers in summer are extremely attractive to honeybees; full sun to part shade, drought tolerant.

Lion's tail (*Leonotis leonurus*). Evergreen shrub native to South Africa, whorls of dark orange flowers attractive to hummingbirds, 4-6 feet, full sun, drought tolerant.

Oregano (*Origanum* spp.). Ornamental and culinary perennials with tiny clusters of flowers attractive to bees and butterflies, needs full sun, drought tolerant. *Origanum laevigatum* 'Herrenhausen' is a popular choice.

Pitcher sages (*Lepechinia calycina, L. fragrans*). Evergreen shrubs loved by bees and hummingbirds, aromatic with fuzzy foliage and white to lavender bell-shaped flowers, 4 feet high, sun to part shade. *Lepechinia fragrans* has showier flowers and lovely fragrance.
- *L. hastata*. This evergreen shrub from Mexico has large pointed leaves and stalks of magenta flowers in summer, up to 6 feet.

Rosemary (*Rosmarinus officinalis*). Profuse blue nectar flowers in late winter for hummers and bees, dense foliage provides cover for ground birds, upright and sprawling forms, full sun, good drainage.

Russian sage (*Perovskia atriplicifolia*). Shrubby perennial with aromatic gray-green foliage and airy sprays of lavender blue flowers late spring/ summer, drought tolerant, needs good drainage and full sun, unappetizing to deer, to 4 feet high.

Sages (*Salvia* spp.). Many native/non-native *Salvia* species to choose from that bloom in different seasons. Essential habitat plants, they feed hummingbirds, bees, butterflies, and other insects. Most sages are ignored by deer.

- Black sage (*S. mellifera*). A bee magnet, this chaparral shrub with dark green foliage blooms with white flowers in spring, low-growing to upright varieties.
- Brandegee sage (*S. brandegeei*). Hardy, easy to grow, this vigorous salvia is similar in appearance to black sage, lavender flowers in early spring, 3-5 ft. tall and wide, needs full sun and a dry site.
- Cleveland sage (*S. clevelandii*). A chaparral shrub with fragrant, summer-blooming dark blue flowers, 3-5 feet tall, needs full sun, drought tolerant. *S.* 'Winifred Gilman' has dark purple flowers, is fast growing and especially aromatic. The cultivar 'Pozo Blue' (hybrid between Cleveland sage and purple sage) is especially attractive to butterflies.
- Creeping sage (*S. sonomensis*). Low-growing groundcover for dry shade, lavender-blue flowers in late spring. *S.* 'Bee's Bliss' has a low, spreading, mounding habit, silvery foliage and blue-lavender flower spikes; great choice for spilling over walls and erosion control.
- Hummingbird sage (*S. spathacea*). Clumping, spreading perennial with whorls of magenta flowers that rise several feet from a base of large, coarse, dark green leaves. This adaptable native salvia takes sun, but prefers part shade; is drought tolerant but readily accepts garden water; especially distasteful to deer.
- Purple sage (*S. leucophylla*). Upright or sprawling shrub good for slopes or spilling over a wall, foliage turns from apple-green to silver in summer, pink to purple flower spikes in spring.
- White sage (*S. apiana*). Native to southern California, this woolly-leafed shrub blooms mostly in summer with white, lavender-tinged flowers.

Non-native sages:

- Autumn sage (*S. greggii*). Hardy evergreen shrub with masses of tiny tubular red, pink, white, or violet flowers summer through fall, full sun/ part shade, 1-4 feet high.
- Clary sage (*S. sclarea*). This strongly scented and very drought-tolerant sage with gray-green, crinkled leaves and tall stalks of creamy flower clusters thrives in hot, dry sites.
- Garden sage (*S. officinalis*). Mediterranean shrub with gray-green foliage and pink, lavender, or white flower spikes in spring and summer, sun, 1-3 feet high.

- Germander sage (*S. chamaedryoides*). Perennial with silvery foliage and blue nectar flowers in summer and fall, works well as a low hedge, good bird habitat, 2 feet x 3-4 feet.
- Pineapple sage (*S. elegans*). Bright red tubular flowers attractive to hummingbirds, pineapple-scented, apple green foliage, hardy but tender perennial, sun, 3-4 feet high.
- Roseleaf sage (*S. involucrata*). Shrubby perennial with large oval leaves and showy dark-fuchsia flowers in late summer, to 5 feet.
- Summer sage (*S. microphylla*). Dense evergreen shrub, many hybrids available. *S. microphylla* 'Hot Lips' forms a thicket with masses of red-and-white flowers from spring through fall, very attractive to bees, 3 x 5 feet.

Thyme (*Thymus* spp.). Shrubby and aromatic Mediterranean perennials for herb gardens, containers, and as groundcover for small areas, sun to part shade, low water, attractive to bees and butterflies.

Plants that need supplemental water

Agastache (*Agastache* spp.). Various summer-blooming species in colors ranging from pink to blue, sun, bee and hummingbird favorite.
- Anise hyssop (*A. foeniculum*). Perennial with heart-shaped foliage and lilac flowers, to 3 feet, leaves for anise-flavored tea, native to North America.

Bee balm (*Monarda didyma*). Spreading, clumping perennial with clusters of tubular flowers in shades of pink, 2-4 feet high, easy to grow, regular water, full sun, very attractive to hummingbirds.

Mint (*Mentha* spp.). Pennyroyal (*M. pulegium*), a creeping perennial with small lavender flowers for moist, shady sites. Culinary mints, such as spearmint (*M. spicata*), peppermint (*M. x piperita*), and others, spread by underground stems and are good candidates for containers; sun to part shade, moderate water. Their tiny flower clusters attract small butterflies and other pollinators.

Sage (*Salvia* spp.).
- Bog sage (*S. uliginosa*). Tall and dense with graceful stems of sky-blue flowers in summer, likes wet feet, good choice for clay soils, bogs or near ponds, 4-6 feet tall, spreads by rhizomes.

Carrot Family (Apiaceae). The umbellifers are top insectary plants providing pollen and nectar for tiny pollinators and beneficial insects. Some members of this family serve as butterfly host plants for the Anise Swallowtail.

Bishop's flower/white lace flower (*Ammi majus*). Annual with ferny foliage and white, lacy umbels, especially attractive to pollinators and beneficial insects, to 2-3 feet high.

Coast angelica (*Angelica hendersonii*). Coastal perennial with stout stems, umbels are white but tighter than the flowers of cow parsnip, 4-6 feet. *A. archangelica*, non-native biennial with large white umbels on tall stems, needs moist soil, butterfly host plant for Anise Swallowtail.

Cow parsnip (*Heracleum lanatum*). Tall, coastal perennial with large, white, flat-topped umbels, attractive to many tiny pollinators and beneficial insects, may be used by the Anise Swallowtail.

Herbs. Plant dill, parsley, culinary fennel, and lovage as food plants for the table, and host plants for the Anise Swallowtail butterfly. Bronze fennel (*Foeniculum* 'Purpurescens' and 'Smokey') has lacy, bronze foliage with yellow umbels and is suitable for gardens.
- Finocchio (*Foeniculum vulgare azoricum*). A culinary fennel grown for its bulb.
- Lovage (*Levisticum officinale*). Resembles a huge celery stalk, about 3 feet high, seeds and leaves are edible.

Pea Family (Fabaeae). The legumes offer nectar and seed and many serve as host plants for butterflies. For many blues and hairstreaks, the pea and buckwheat families are the only source of caterpillar food plants.

Alfalfa (*Medicago sativa*), clovers (*Trifolium* spp.), and vetch (*Vicia* spp.— many are invasive) are butterfly host plants for blues, hairstreaks, and other common butterfly species in California.

Fairy duster (*Calliandra californica*). Evergreen to summer-deciduous shrub with fluffy pink blossoms very attractive to hummingbirds, full sun, drought tolerant, combines nicely with succulents. Brazilian flame bush (*C. tweedii*) is native to Brazil, fluffy scarlet flowers very attractive to hummers, 6-8 feet tall, drought tolerant, best with heat and warm winters.

Lotus (*Lotus* spp.). Native and non-native species.
- Deerweed (*L. scoparius*). Small perennial common to chaparral plant communities, yellow flowers, full sun and no supplemental water once established, butterfly host plant for the Orange Sulfur, Acmon Blue, Silvery Blue, and Northern Cloudywing.

Lupine (*Lupinus* spp.). Shrubs and perennials with great wildlife value— seeds for quail and other bird species, nectar for pollinators. Butterfly host plants for Arrowhead Blue, Silvery Blue, Melissa Blue, Orange Sulfur.

Sweet pea (*Lathyrus* spp.). Native and non-native species, butterfly host plant for Western Tailed-Blue.

Buckwheat Family (Polygonaceae). Important as food, nectar, and butterfly host plants, drought-tolerant buckwheats also provide rich sources of pollen for bees and beneficial insects, and cover and seeds for birds. Over 100 species of buckwheat are native to California; they are found on coastal bluffs and rocky hillsides and numerous other habitats in well-drained, sandy soil. Species vary from large and small shrubs to herbaceous perennials. Most buckwheat species bloom in late summer and fall. Foliage is usually gray-green and flowers are white to rosy brown. Plant in full sun and combine with seaside daisy, succulents, California aster, and other perennials of the coastal scrub plant community.

Ashyleaf buckwheat (*Eriogonum cinereum*). Small shrub with clusters of soft-pink flowers from summer through winter, no water in coastal areas but may need occasional water inland. Native to southern California.

California buckwheat (*E. fasciculatum*). Widespread, shrubby perennial with white to pink flowers from late spring through fall, 3 x 4 feet, butterfly host plant for Acmon Blue and Square-spotted Blue.

Channel Island buckwheats. The following buckwheat species from the Channel Islands grow in windy, salty air and prefer dry, clay soil and no summer water once established, good choice for coastal or dry gardens.
- Red buckwheat (*E. grande* var. *rubescens*). Native perennial from coastal sage scrub of southern California, reddish-pink flowers, very attractive in drifts, 1-3 feet tall.
- St. Catherine's lace (*E. giganteum*). Largest of the buckwheats with very attractive lacy white flower clusters, to 6 feet tall and 6 feet wide, full sun, drought tolerant.
- Santa Cruz Island buckwheat (*E. arborescens*). Bushy shrub with pink- to cream-colored flower clusters on long stems from May to September, 3-5 feet tall, good choice for southern coastal California gardens.

Coast buckwheat (*E. latifolium*). Low-growing perennial with white to pink flower clusters that turn to shades of rust in fall. This buckwheat is water tolerant, needs full sun, lean soils, good choice for coastal gardens. Native to southern California and butterfly host plant for the Green Hairstreak.

Conejo buckwheat (*E. crocatum*). Rare and endangered buckwheat that blooms in summer with flat, sulfur-yellow flower clusters that fade to rusty orange, good choice for rock gardens or containers. Native to southern California.

Sulfur buckwheat (*E. umbellatum*). Large sulfur-yellow flower clusters that fade to rust contrast with gray-green, low-mounding foliage; native to dry, rocky slopes, good choice for inland rock gardens.

Snapdragon Family (Scrophularia). The figworts are important nectar plants for hummingbirds, bees, and other pollinators. They provide seeds and cover for birds and some members of this family serve as host plants for butterflies.

Bee plant (*Scrophularia californica*). Tall perennial with tiny red flower clusters resembling miniature orchids atop long stems, 3-6 feet high, easy to grow in sun to light shade, best with some moisture, attractive to bees and hummers, butterfly host plant for the Variable Checkerspot.

Heart-leaved penstemon (*Keckiella cordifolia*). A climbing shrub with scarlet flowers in late spring/summer, full sun or part shade, frost tender, 5 feet or higher, native to the Channel Islands. Yellow bush penstemon (*K. antirrhinoides*) has an upright spreading habit to 4 feet, fragrant yellow flowers in summer, native to southern California. (*Note: Keckiella* species, and most of the other scrophs, were recently moved to the Plantain family.)

Monkeyflowers (*Mimulus* spp.). The tubular flowers of monkeyflower species are favorites of hummingbirds.
- Bush monkeyflower (*M. aurantiacus*). Evergreen, shrubby perennial that grows on coastal bluffs and rocky inland areas, yellow-orange flowers (hybrids of many colors), full sun to part shade, drought tolerant, butterfly host plant for the Variable Checkerspot. Combine bush monkeyflower with native salvias or other drought-tolerant native shrubs.
- Creek (seep) monkeyflower (*M. guttatus*). Herbaceous perennial with bright yellow tubular flowers spring and summer, dormant in winter, self-sows readily, found along seeps and streams, butterfly host plant for Common Buckeye; needs full sun and summer water, good bog plant.
- Red monkeyflower (*M. puniceus*). Southern California native similar to bush monkeyflower but with scarlet flowers, 3-4 feet high, full sun, best with some summer water.
- Scarlet monkeyflower (*M. cardinalis*). This orange-flowered monkeyflower is a good choice for bogs or other moist spots.

Mullein (*Verbascum* spp.). Biennials and perennials with tall spikes of yellow flowers (most species) and soft, woolly, gray-green leaves, self-seed, need full sun, dry or moist soil.

Penstemon (*Penstemon* spp.). Many native and non-native species, easy-to-grow perennials with long-blooming flowers of many colors. *Penstemon* species are sometimes used by the Common Buckeye butterfly as host plants.
- Foothill penstemon (*P. heterophyllus*). Low-growing perennial with blue flowers in spring and summer, little to no summer water. 'Margarita BOP' is a popular and hardy cultivar.
- Royal penstemon (*P. spectabilis*). Native to southern California, dark rose-colored flowers in spring, 3-4 feet tall.
- Scarlet bugler (*P. centranthifolius*). Native to dry, sunny chaparral communities, scarlet-red flowers on stalks to 3 feet high, needs good drainage.
- Scented penstemon (*P. palmeri*). Native perennial from the Southwest, very fragrant pale lavender flowers, needs dry, hot conditions, suitable for desert gardens.

Snapdragon (*Antirrhinum majus*). Many varieties and flower colors available, regular summer water, sun or part shade, caterpillar host plants for the Common Buckeye butterfly. (*Note: Antirrhinum* species, and most other scrophs, were recently moved to the Plantain family.)

Toadflax (*Linaria purpurea*). Tiny, pale pink to violet snapdragon flowers on wispy stems from spring through fall, to 3 feet tall, host plant for Common Buckeye butterfly.

Mallow Family (Malvaceae). Easy-to-grow shrubs and perennials for sunny areas, members of the mallow family serve as butterfly host plants and nectar plants for butterflies and other pollinators. Birds eat the seeds and the insects they attract.

Chaparral mallow (*Malacothamnus fasciculatus*). Fast-growing, hardy, dense evergreen shrub with soft gray-green foliage and lovely, pale pink flowers in early summer, 3-10 feet high, sun or part shade, drought tolerant. Combine with sage, buckwheat, coyote mint, and other chaparral plants, good choice for banks and erosion control.

Checkerbloom (*Sidalcea malviflora*). A perennial wildflower with pink hollyhock-like flowers in spring, generally 8 inches high (some taller varieties). Mix with annual and perennial wildflowers and bunchgrasses in a meadow garden or grow in a container.

Desert mallow (*Sphaeralcea ambigua*). This drought-tolerant shrub blooms with many flowers in shades of orange and red, 3-4 feet tall. Combine with succulents in desert gardens.

Flowering maple (*Abutilon* spp.). Upright, airy evergreen shrub with maple-leafed foliage and bell-shaped flowers in red, orange, yellow, and white that bloom almost continuously, sun to part shade, very attractive to hummingbirds. Indian mallow (*A. palmeri*) is a drought-tolerant shrub for southern California gardens with soft, heart-shaped leaves and clusters of yellow-orange flowers in spring.

Hollyhock (*Alcea rosea*). Old-fashioned hollyhocks come in many beautiful colors, tall, single varieties best nectar plants, may be used by the West Coast Lady butterfly as a host plant.

Tree mallow (*Lavatera* spp.). Mostly evergreen shrubs with hollyhock-like flowers in shades of pink, maple-shaped leaves. Island mallow (*Lavatera/Malva assurgentiflora*). Evergreen shrub native to Channel Islands, large rose-colored flowers from spring through fall, to 10 feet tall, needs full sun and occasional water.

Verbena Family (Verbenaceae). Members of the verbena family are top butterfly nectar plants. Plant verbena species in drifts to attract butterflies and other pollinators. Birds eat the seeds and the insects the plants attract.

Chaste tree (*Vitex agnus-castus*). Fast-growing deciduous shrub or small tree with beautiful foliage and large fragrant spikes of dark lavender flowers similar to those of buddleia, full sun, some summer water, very deer resistant.

Lantana (*Lantana* spp.). Mounding or trailing evergreen shrubs with many clusters of small flowers in lavender, yellow, or white that bloom almost continuously in frost-free areas. Highly valued as nectar plants for butterflies and bees, full sun, low water, deer proof.

Lemon verbena (*Aloysia triphylla*). A leggy shrub that grows to 6 x 6 feet, lemon-scented leaves for tea, white nectar flowers for pollinators and other insects, sun to part shade, summer water as needed.

Verbenas (*Verbena* spp.). Summer-blooming annuals and perennials in clusters of pink flowers very attractive to butterflies and other pollinators.
- Cedros island verbena (*V. lilacina*). Small, evergreen shrub native to Baja California, lacy green foliage with lilac flowers most of the year, needs heat and full sun. 'De La Mina' has darker flowers.
- *V. bonariensis*. Native to South America, this tall, airy perennial blooms from summer to fall with clusters of fragrant, tiny pink-lavender flowers, 3-6 feet tall, hosts ladybird beetles, more effective when massed in drifts. Plant seeds outdoors in early spring in full sun and cover with 1/4 inch of soil; reseeds freely.
- *V. hastata*. This native perennial has an upright growth habit with multiple spikes of pink-lavender flowers. Though often found in marshy areas, this plant is drought tolerant.
- *V. rigida*. Short perennial with lilac flowers to 2 feet, very effective nectar plant when massed in drifts.
- *V. officinalis*. Vervain is a woody perennial and garden herb, tiny pale lilac flowers in summer, good for sunny, dry sites, needs well-drained soil.

APPENDIX H

Invasive Pest Plants

Through a combination of genetic aggressiveness and an absence of natural checks and balances, exotic pest plants have out-competed native bunchgrasses, wildflowers, and many other indigenous plants. Colonizing and weaving their way through coastal lands, forests, meadows, even riparian areas, many of these pest plants are commonly found in gardens or easily available in nurseries. Too often, pest plants escape garden boundaries into open space, where they gradually take over a site, weakening the health of the native ecosystem and its ability to support local wildlife. Help protect the diversity and integrity of ecosystems that have developed over thousands of years by not planting "invasives." Below are some of the most pernicious invasive plants. For more information on California's invasive plant problem, visit the California Invasive Plant Council at www.cal-ipc.org.

Cotoneasters (*Cotoneaster lacteus, C. pannosus*). Birds spread the seeds to many habitats where this fast-growing plant quickly displaces native flora. *A better choice*: Plant non-invasive toyon (*Heteromeles arbutifolia*), a large, native evergreen shrub or tree with bright red berries that feed birds in winter.

Gorse (*Ulex europea*) and Spanish broom (*Spartium junceum*), French broom (*Genista monspessulana*), Scotch broom (*Cytisus scoparius*), Portuguese broom (*C. striatus*).

Spanish broom was offered in nurseries starting in the late 1850s; Scotch broom and French broom soon followed. Like most invasive exotics they were easy to cultivate, produced abundant seed, and adapted to our climate. They have taken over one million acres in California. Gorse, similar to the brooms, has replaced whole plant communities in grasslands along the coast. They have little wildlife value and are also fire hazards.

Japanese dodder (*Cuscuta japonica*). This fast-growing parasitic vine, which rapidly spreads from one host plant to another, is bright yellow and leafless. Trees, shrubs, and ground plants are all vulnerable to attack.

Licorice plant (*Helichrysum petiolare*). Commonly planted in gardens, this perennial has smothered wildflowers and many other indigenous plants over a large area of Mount Tamalpais in the San Francisco Bay Region, while invading other coastal areas as well.

Pampas grass (*Cortaderia selloana*). These enormous plants, which are fire hazards, have disrupted wild habitat throughout many areas of California. *A better choice*: Plant native deergrass (*Muhlenbergia rigens*), a large, native bunchgrass with tall flower spikes, as a drought-tolerant alternative for gardens and steep, sunny banks.

Periwinkle (*Vinca major*), English ivy (*Hedera helix*), Algerian ivy (*H. canariensis*), South African capeweed (*Arctotheca calendula*), cape ivy (*Delairea odorata*). These aggressive groundcovers spread rapidly in shaded woodlands invading creek banks and other riparian sites where they smother native plants. The waxy foliage of cape ivy is distasteful to wildlife and may be harmful to fish as well. *A better choice*: Native groundcovers such as wild ginger (*Asarum caudatum*), California pipevine (*Aristolochia californica*), and stream sedge (*Carex nudata*), which offer cover and food for birds and insects, are suitable for shady, riparian sites.

Scarlet wisteria (*Sesbania punicea*) is an especially pernicious plant that is often found along creeks and streams. (See Appendix B, Native Plant Communities, for streamside plant alternatives.)

APPENDIX I

Sources of California Native Plants

California Native Plant Society: www.cnps.org
> Check with local chapters for meetings, field trips, annual garden tours, and plant sales

Northern California Nurseries

Berkeley Horticultural Nursery
1310 McGee Ave., Berkeley, CA 94703
(510) 526-4704
www.berkeleyhort.com

California Flora Nursery
Somers & D Streets, Fulton, CA 95439
(707) 528-8813
www.calfloranursery.com
> Habitat gardening focus; most plants propagated and grown on site

Central Coast Wilds (by appointment)
336 A Golf Club Dr., Santa Cruz, CA 95060
(831) 459-0655
www.centralcoastwilds.com
> Ecological restoration consulting

Cornflower Farms (wholesale only, by appointment)
9811 Sheldon Rd., Elk Grove, CA 95759
(916) 689-1015
www.cornflowerfarms.com

Elkhorn Native Plant Nursery
1957B Hwy 1, Moss Landing, CA 95039
(831) 763-1207
www.elkhornnursery.com

Freshwater Farms, Inc.
5851 Myrtle Ave., Eureka, CA 95503
(800) 200-8969
www.freshwaterfarms.com
> Wetland and riparian California natives/seeds

In the spring the flowers of Brandegee sage (*Salvia brandegeei*) are a magnet for bees and other pollinators.
PHOTOGRAPH BY MIEKO WATKINS.

Mostly Natives Nursery
27235 Hwy. 1, Tomales, CA 94971
(707) 878-2009
www.mostlynatives.com
    Butterfly and hummingbird plant lists

Native Here Nursery (call ahead)
Tilden Regional Park
101 Golf Course Dr., Berkeley, CA 94708
(510) 549-0211
www.ebcnps.org

Native Revival Nursery
2600 Mar Vista Dr., Aptos, CA 95003
(831) 684-1811
www.nativerevival.com

Rana Creek Nursery
35351 E. Carmel Valley Rd., Carmel Valley, CA 93924
(831) 659-2830
www.ranacreeknursery.com
    Habitat restoration services

Sierra Azul Nursery
2660 East Lake Ave., Watsonville, CA 95076
(831) 763-0939
www.sierraazul.com
    Specializing in natives and other Mediterranean climate plants

Sonoma Horticultural Nursery
3970 Azalea Ave., Sebastopol, CA 95472
(707) 823-6832
www.sonomahort.com
    Extensive woodland demo garden; shade-loving plants,
    including some natives

The Watershed Nursery
601-A Canal Blvd., Richmond, CA 94804
(510) 234-2222
www.thewatershednursery.com

Yerba Buena Nursery
19500 Skyline Blvd., Woodside, CA 94062
(650) 851-1668
www.yerbabuenanursery.com
    Large demo garden

Southern California Nurseries

Las Pilitas Nursery
3232 Las Pilitas Rd., Santa Margarita, CA 93453
(805) 438-5992
and
8331 Nelson Way, Escondido, CA 92026
(760) 749-5932
www.laspilitas.com
Extensive information on growing natives and creating wildlife habitats

Native Sons Nursery
379 West El Campo Rd., Arroyo Grande, CA 93420
(805) 481-5996
www.nativeson.com

Theodore Payne Foundation
10459 Tuxford St., Sun Valley, CA 91352
(818) 768-1802
www.theodorepayne.org
Large demo garden and nature trail; workshops; seeds available online; annual garden tour

Tree of Life Nursery
33201 Ortega Hwy, San Juan Capistrano, CA 92693
(949) 728-0685
www.californianativeplants.com
Extensive information on natives and habitat gardening

Grasses

California Native Grasslands Association: www.cnga.org
Advocacy group for preserving and restoring California's native grasses, guide to California's grasslands

Hedgerow Farms
21740 County Road 88, Winters, CA 95694
(530) 662-6847
www.hedgerowfarms.com
California native grasses and seeds

Pacific Coast Seed
533 Hawthorne Place, Livermore, CA 94550
(925) 373-4417
www.pcseed.com
Native heritage grasses

Native Plant Seeds

ConservaSeed
P.O. Box 455, Rio Vista, CA 94571
(916) 775-1676
Gasses and legumes; restoration and revegetation

Clyde Robin Seed Co.
P.0. Box 2366, Castro Valley, CA 94546
(510) 785-0425

Larner Seeds
P.O. Box 407, Bolinas, CA 94924
(415) 868-9407
www.larnerseeds.com
Extensive seed list, especially wildflowers and mixes; demo garden; backyard restoration services

Native Seeds/SEARCH: www.nativeseeds.org

Note: For additional sources of native plants, see www.plantnative.com

Botanic Gardens for Inspiration and Seasonal Native Plant Sales

The Gardens at Heather Farms
1540 Marchbanks Dr., Walnut Creek, CA 94598
(925) 947-1678
www.gardenshf.org
Native plant demonstration garden

Hallberg Butterfly Gardens
8687 Oak Grove Avenue, Sebastopol, CA 95472
(707) 823-3420
www.hallbergbutterflygardens.org
Note: Open by appointment only, April–October

The Occidental Arts & Ecology Center
15290 Coleman Valley Rd., Occidental, CA 95465
(707) 874-1557
www.oaec.org
Semi-annual plant sales of heirloom vegetables and flowers; extensive food gardens; permaculture classes; plant sales; not open for drop-in visitors

Rancho Santa Ana Botanic Garden
1500 N. College Ave., Claremont, CA 91711
(909) 625-8767
www.rsabg.org

Regional Parks Botanic Garden
Tilden Regional Park
Wildcat Canyon Rd./South Park Dr., Berkeley, CA 94708
(510) 544-3169
www.nativeplants.org
    Annual plant sale third Saturday in April; by appointment on Thursday
    mornings

San Francisco Botanical Garden
Golden Gate Park
9th Ave. at Lincoln Way, San Francisco, CA 94122
(415) 661-1316
www.sfbotanicalgarden.org
    California native plant section

Santa Barbara Botanic Garden
1212 Mission Canyon Rd., Santa Barbara, CA 93105
(805) 682-4726
www.sbbg.org

University of California Botanical Garden at Berkeley
200 Centennial Dr., Berkeley, CA 94720
(510) 643-2755
www.botanicalgarden.berkeley.edu
    California native plant section; native plants available

APPENDIX J
Books and Resources

California Natives/Photos and Database

Calflora: www.calflora.org

CalPhotos: www.calphotos.berkeley.edu/flora
Comprehensive California database and photos of native plants (and non-native species that grow wild in California).

Reference Books

Beidleman, Linda H. and Eugene N. Kozloff. *Plants of the San Francisco Bay Region.* Pacific Grove, CA: Sagen Press, 1994.

East Bay Municipal Utility District Staff. *Plants and Landscapes for Summer-Dry Climates of the San Francisco Bay Region.* Oakland, CA: EBMUD, 2004. www.ebmud.com.
Highly recommended. Many good wildlife habitat plants among hundreds of carefully selected low-water-use plants; stunning garden visuals; native plant communities and basic gardening information for growing a healthy, water-conserving garden.

Perry, Bob. *Landscape Plants for Western Regions.* Claremont, CA: Land Design Publishing, 1992.

Garden Ecology

Buchmann, Stephen L. and Gary Paul Nabhan. *The Forgotten Pollinators.* Washington, DC: Island Press, 1996.

Carroll, Steven B. and Steven D. Salt. *Ecology for Gardeners.* Portland, OR: Timber Press, 2004.
Entomologists and long-time gardeners offer thorough exploration of the garden as mini-ecoystem.

Francis, Mark and Andreas Reimann. *The California Landscape Garden: Ecology, Culture, and Design.* Berkeley, CA: University of California Press, 1999.

Greenlee, John. *The American Meadow Garden.* Portland, OR: Timber Press, 2009.

Grissell, Eric. *Insects and Gardens.* Portland, OR: Timber Press, 2001.

Hemenway, Toby. *Gaia's Garden: A Guide to Home-Scale Permaculture.* White River Junction, VT: Chelsea Green Publishing Company, 2001.

Lovejoy, Ann. *Ann Lovejoy's Organic Garden Design School.* Emmaus, PA: Rodale, Inc., 2001.

Covers all the basics of designing and maintaining a healthy and beautiful garden with a reader-friendly and common sense approach. Lovejoy runs a gardening school on Bainbridge Island near Seattle, has authored more than 18 books, and is considered one of the country's leading garden experts.

Stein, Sara. *Noah's Garden: Restoring the Ecology of Our Own Backyards.* Boston, MA: Houghton Mifflin Co., 1993.

Tallamy, Douglas. *Bringing Nature Home.* Portland, OR: Timber Press, 2007.

A gardener and entomologist, Tallamy makes a convincing case for turning our gardens into wildlife-friendly sanctuaries. His lucid, reader-friendly style and often fascinating examples clarify the connection between native plants and wildlife.

Tallamy, Douglas. *Bringing Nature Home: How You Can Sustain Wildlife with Native Plants.* Portland, OR: Timber Press, 2009.

Wasowski, Andy and Sally Wasowski. *The Landscaping Revolution.* Chicago, IL: Contemporary Books, 2000.

Gardening with Native Plants

Bornstein, Carol, David Fross, and Bart O'Brien. *California Native Plants for the Garden.* Los Olivos, CA: Cachuma Press, 2005.

Keator, Glenn and Alrie Middlebrook. *Designing California Native Gardens.* Berkeley, CA: University of California Press, 2007.

Lowry, Judith Larner. *Gardening with a Wild Heart: Restoring California's Native Landscapes at Home.* Berkeley, CA: University of California, 1999.

Parker, Reny. *Wildflowers of Northern California's Wine Country & North Coast Ranges.* Cloverdale, CA: New Creek Ranch Press, 2007.

Schmidt, Marjorie. *Growing California Native Plants.* Berkeley, CA: University of California Press, 1980.

Smith, Nevin. *Native Treasures.* Berkeley, CA: University of California Press, 2006.

Van Atta, Susan. *The Southern California Native Flower Garden.* Salt Lake City, UT: Gibbs Smith, 2009.

Reader-friendly guide to native plants suitable for southern California gardens; includes wildlife value, growing requirements, and companionable plants for the garden.

Wildlife Guides and Resources

Allen, Thomas J., Jim P. Brock, and Jeffrey Glassberg. *Caterpillars in the Field and Garden: A Field Guide to the Butterfly Caterpillars of North America.* New York, NY: Oxford University Press, 2005.

Biggs, Kathy. *Common Dragonflies of California*, revised edition. Sebastopol, CA: Azalea Creek Publishing, 2009.

Dunn, Jon L. and Jonathan Alderfer. *National Geographic Field Guide to the Birds of North America*, Sixth Edition. Washington, DC: National Geographic Society, 2011

Ehrlich, Paul R., David S. Dobkin, and Darryl Wheye. *The Birder's Handbook.* New York, NY: Simon & Schuster, 1988.

Glassberg, Jeffrey. *Butterflies through Binoculars: The West: A Field Guide to the Butterflies of Western North America.* New York, NY: Oxford University Press, 2001.

Manolis, Tim. *Dragonflies and Damselflies of California.* Berkeley, CA: University of California Press, 2003.

O'Brien, Stacey. *Wesley the Owl: The Remarkable Love Story of an Owl and His Girl.* New York, NY: Free Press, 2008.

Paulson, Dennis. *Dragonflies and Damselflies of the West.* Princeton, NJ: Princeton University Press, 2009.

Powell, Jerry A. and Charles L. Hogue. *California Insects.* Berkeley, CA: University of California Press, 1979.

Shapiro, Arthur M. and Timothy D. Manolis. *Field Guide to the Butterflies of the San Francisco Bay and Sacramento Valley Regions.* Berkeley, CA: University of California Press, 2007.

Sibley, David Allen. *The Sibley Guide to Birds.* New York, NY: Alfred A. Knopf, 2000.

Sibley, David Allen, Chris Elphick, and John. B. Dunning, Jr. *The Sibley Guide to Bird Life and Behavior.* New York, NY: Alfred A. Knopf, 2001.

Stewart, Bob. *Common Butterflies of California.* Patagonia, AZ: West Coast Lady Press, 1997.
    Highly recommended, though out of print. Full page color photos and host plants; worth searching for in bookstores or libraries.

Websites for Gardening with Wildlife

CALIFORNIA-BASED WEBSITES

Build a Wildlife Pond: www.bigsnestpond.net/BuildPond.html

California Bat Conservation Fund: www.californiabats.com
Staff offers information on California bats, presentations for schools and organizations and bat house instructions.

Growing Native, Louise Lacey: www.growingnative.com
Growing Native, published for ten years, is now available as segments that can be downloaded: The Basics of Growing Native and the Plant Communities; Perennials; Shrubs; and Wildlife and Inspiration. $15 each.

Hungry Owl Project: www.hungryowl.org

PRBO Conservation Science: www.prbo.org
Landscaping recommendations, protection from cats and other predators, windows, bird feeders, nest boxes, and more.

Urban Bee Gardens, Gordon Frankie, UC Berkeley:
www.nature.berkeley.edu/urbanbeegardens

General Information

National Wildlife Federation: www.nwf.org

NWF's Backyard Habitat Certification Program:
www.nwf.org/gardenforwildlife

Nature Conservancy

Cornell Birdhouse Network: www.birds.cornell.edu/birdhouse

Cornell Laboratory of Ornithology: www.AllAboutBirds.org

Enature: www.enature.com
Backyard habitat gardening information

Monarch Watch Waystation Program: www.monarchwatch.org

National Audubon Society: www.audubon.org

North American Butterfly Association (NABA): www.naba.org

Xerces Society: www.xerces.org

Resources for Creating Schoolyard Wildlife Habitat

Danks, Sharon. *Asphalt to Ecosystems: Design Ideas for Schoolyard Transformation.* Oakland, CA: New Village Press, 2010.

National Wildlife Federation, Schoolyard Habitats: www.nwf.org/schoolyard

Heirloom Flowers, Vegetables and Herbs, Old-Fashioned Annuals and Perennials

Abundant Life Seed Foundation: www.abundantlifeseeds.com

Annie's Annuals and Perennials: www.anniesannuals.com
    Many heirloom varieties of nectar flowers and native wildflowers

Baker Creek Heirloom Seeds: www.rareseeds.com

Bountiful Gardens (Ecology Action): www.bountifulgardens.org

J.L. Hudson, Seedsman: www.jlhudsonseeds.net

Peaceful Valley Farm and Garden Supply: www.GrowOrganic.com

Seedhunt: www.seedhunt.com

Seeds of Change: www.seedsofchange.com

Seed Savers Exchange: www.seedsavers.org

Territorial Seed Company: www.territorialseed.com

Integrated Pest Management

Beyond Pesticides: www.beyondpesticides.org

Bio-Integral Resource Center: www.birc.org

Directory of Least-Toxic Pest Control Products, The IPM Practitioner, BIRC, (510) 524-1758, birc@igc.org

Northwest Coalition for Alternatives to Pesticides: www.pesticide.org

UC Statewide IPM: www.ipm.ucdavis.edu/PMG/menu.homegarden.html

Bibliography

Allen, Thomas J., Jim P. Brock, and Jeffrey Glassberg. 2005. *Caterpillars in the Field and Garden: A Field Guide to the Butterfly Caterpillars of North America.* New York, NY: Oxford University Press.

Altizer, Sonia and Jaap de Roode. "When Butterflies Get Bugs: The ABCs of Lepidopteran Disease." *American Butterflies*, Vol. 18, No. 2 (Summer 2010): 16–26.

Bauer, Nancy. 2008. *The Habitat Garden Book: Wildlife Landscaping for the San Francisco Bay Region.* Sebastopol, CA: Coyote Ridge Press.

Beidleman, Linda H. and Eugene N. Kozloff. 1994. *Plants of the San Francisco Bay Region.* Pacific Grove, CA: Sagen Press.

Biggs, Kathy. 2000. *Common Dragonflies of California.* Sebastopol, CA: Azalea Creek Publishing.

Bornstein, Carol, David Fross, and Bart O'Brien. 2007. *California Native Plants for the Garden.* Los Olivos, CA: Cachuma Press.

Borror, Donald J. and Richard E. White. 1970. *Insects.* Peterson Field Guides. Boston: Houghton Mifflin Co.

Brenzel, Kathleen Norris, ed. 2001. *Sunset Western Garden Book.* Menlo Park, CA: Sunset Publishing Corporation.

Buchmann, Stephen L. and Gary Paul Nabhan. 1996. *The Forgotten Pollinators.* Washington, DC: Island Press.

Carroll, Steven B. and Steven D. Salt. 2004. *Ecology for Gardeners.* Portland, OR: Timber Press.

Clebsch, Betsy. 2003. *The New Book of Salvias: Sages for Every Garden.* Portland, OR: Timber Press.

Daniels, Stevie.1995. *The Wild Lawn Handbook: Alternatives to the Traditional Front Lawn.* New York, NY: MacMillan, Inc.

East Bay Municipal Utility District Staff. 2004. *Plants and Landscapes for Summer-Dry Climates of the San Francisco Bay Region.* Oakland, CA: EBMUD.

Evans, Arthur V. and James N. Hogue. 2004. *Introduction to California Beetles.* Berkeley, CA: University of California Press.

Francis, Mark, and Andreas Reimann. 1999. *The California Landscape Garden.* Berkeley and Los Angeles, CA: University of California Press.

Frankie, Gordon W., Robbin W. Thorp, Mary H. Schindler, Barbara Ertter, and Margaret Przybylski. "Bees in Berkeley?" *Fremontia*, Vol. 30, Nos. 3-4 (2002): 50–58.

Garth, John S. and J.W. Tilden. 1986. *California Butterflies*. Berkeley, CA: University of California Press.

Greenlee, John. 2009. *The American Meadow Garden*. Portland, OR: Timber Press.

Grissell, Eric. 2001. *Insects and Gardens*. Portland, OR: Timber Press.

Hamilton, Geoff. 1995. *The Organic Garden Book*. New York, NY: Dorling Kindersley, Inc.

Hemenway, Toby. 2001. *Gaia's Garden: A Guide to Home-Scale Permaculture*. White River Junction, VT: Chelseas Green Publishing Co.

Keator, Glenn. 1990. *Complete Garden Guide to the Native Perennials of California*. San Francisco, CA: Chronicle Books.

Keator, Glenn. 1994. *Complete Garden Guide to the Native Shrubs of California*. San Francisco, CA: Chronicle Books.

Keator, Glenn and Alrie Middlebrook. 2007. *Designing California Native Gardens: The Plant Community Approach to Artful, Ecological Gardens*. Berkeley, CA: University of California Press.

Link, Russell. 2000. *Landscaping for Wildlife in the Pacific Northwest*. Seattle, WA: University of Washington Press & Washington Department of Fish and Wildlife.

Lowry, Judith Larner. 1999. *Gardening with a Wild Heart: Restoring California's Native Landscapes at Home*. Berkeley, CA: University of California Press.

Muir, John. 1894. *The Mountains of California*. Excerpt from *The Bee-Pastures* by John Muir, published by Partners for Sustainable Pollination (2009).

Nash, Helen. 1994. *The Pond Doctor*. New York, NY: Sterling Publishing, Inc.

National Geographic Society. 1987. *Field Guide to the Birds of North America*, Second Edition. Washington, DC: National Geographic Society.

Oberhauser, Karen S. and Michelle J. Solensky, editors. 2004. *The Monarch Butterfly: Biology and Conservation*. Ithaca, NY: Cornell University Press.

Ondra, Nancy J. 2002. *Grasses*. North Adams, MA: Storey Publishing.

Pavlik, Bruce and others. 2002. *Oaks of California*. Los Olivos, CA: Cachuma Press and the California Oak Foundation.

Powell, Jerry A. and Charles L. Hogue. 1979. *California Insects*. Berkeley, CA: University of California Press.

Russell, Sabin. "Lizards Slow Lyme Disease in West: Ticks bite them—and leave with purified blood." *San Francisco Chronicle*. April 17, 1998.

Schmidt, Marjorie G. 1980. *Growing California Native Plants*. Berkeley, CA: University of California Press.

Shapiro, Arthur M. "Are Butterflies in Trouble? If So, Why?" *News of the Lepidopterists' Society*, Vol. 52, No. 1, pp. 10–14, Spring 2010.

Shapiro, Arthur M. "Butterfly Monitoring: On Being in the Right Place at the Right Time," *Wings* (2010), pp. 8–13.

Smith, Nevin M. 2006. *Native Treasures*. Berkeley, CA: University of California Press.

Stewart, Bob. 1998. *Common Butterflies of California*. Patagonia, AZ: West Coast Lady Press.

Tallamy, Douglas W. 2007. *Bringing Nature Home: How Native Plants Sustain Wildlife in Our Gardens*. Portland, OR: Timber Press.

Tallamy, Douglas W. 2009. *Bringing Nature Home: How You Can Sustain Wildlife with Native Plants*. Portland, OR: Timber Press.

Van Atta, Susan. 2009. *The Southern California Native Flower Garden*. Layton, UT: Gibbs Smith.

Waldbauer, Gilbert. 2000. *Millions of Monarchs, Bunches of Beetles: How Bugs Find Strength in Numbers*. Cambridge, MA: Harvard University Press.

Wasowski, Andy and Sally Wasowski. 2000. *The Landscaping Revolution*. Chicago, IL: Contemporary Books.

Wright, Amy Bartlett. 1993. *Peterson First Guides: Caterpillars*. Boston, MA: Houghton Mifflin Co.

WEBSITES

The Attra Project, National Sustainable Agriculture Information, University of Arkansas, Fayetteville: www.attra.org/attra-pub/nativebee.html

California Bat Conservation Fund: www.californiabats.com

California Oak Foundation: www.californiaoaks.org

Gordon Frankie, professor at UC Berkeley: www.nature.Berkeley.ed/urbanbeegardens–seasonal recommended plant lists

Monarch Watch, Kansas Biological Survey, University of Kansas: www.monarchwatch.org

North American Butterfly Association: www.naba.org

Pt. Reyes Bird Observatory (PRBO): www.prbo.org

PRBO Conservation Science/ California Partners in Flight published reports: www.prbo/btbf/Backyard.html#limits, 2000:

http://www.prbo.org/calpif/pdfs/riparian_v-2.pdf

http://www.prbo.org/calpif/plans.html

http://www.prbo.org/cms/docs/observer/focus/focus29cats1991.pdf

http://www.prbo.org/cms/56

World Wildlife Fund: www.worldwildlife.org

Gray squirrel.
PHOTOGRAPH
BY ROBERT WATKINS.

Plant Index

Note: Bold indicates pages with photographs